Studies in Social and Cultural Anthropology

Kulturstiftung Sibirien

Studies in Social and Cultural Anthropology

Tatiana Safonova and István Sántha

Evenki microcosm

Visual analysis of hunter-gatherers' lifestyles in eastern Siberia

Verlag der Kulturstiftung Sibirien
SEC Publications

This publication was supported by the
Russian Foundation for Basic Research (RFBR),
research project 18-59-23007

РФФИ

Bibliografische Informationen der Deutschen Nationalbibliothek:
Die Deutsche Nationalbibliothek verzeichnet diese Publikation in der
Deutschen Nationalbibliografie: detaillierte bibliografische Daten sind im Internet über
<http://dnb.d-nb.de> abrufbar.

Cover photo:
Tatiana Safonova and István Sántha

Typesetting:
Kulturstiftung Sibirien gGmbH, Fürstenberg/Havel

Printer:
Books on Demand GmbH, Norderstedt

Electronic edition: https://dh-north.org/publikationen/evenki-microcosm
ISBN: 978-3-942883-36-8

Table of contents

Introduction

Most memorable moments in the field are very personal, which you have no means to put into words and sharing with your colleagues from academia. You sit in a hut after a difficult day, when you are starved, you've worked hard, walked many kilometres and carried heavy weights. There is silence and the only sound is the fire in the stove. You do not talk, you do not have the desire or energy to ask anything, and you do not know what to ask, because you shared this road and this day. And although no verbal information is exchanged during this evening, you feel like you are full of information of another sort. But you do not have the means to register it, put it into the diary and then share it through citations in your articles. These valuable moments happen often, they give you the authority to speak as if you know the culture, these people, those animals and that environment. If you reach these moments when you do not want to talk, and your informants do not want to talk to you either, you get a certain feeling of being embedded in the situation you are studying. After these moments, your body posture changes a little bit, your intonations unconsciously start to mimic those who surround you, your real fieldwork starts. But this is precisely the point when you slowly stop writing your diary, because without much talking, you do not have much to write about. These most precious moments stay outside of research and fieldwork notes, the nonverbal knowledge transferred during these silent periods is never transcribed and put down on paper. In this book we propose a challenging way to grasp these nonverbal messages and document them.

Gregory Bateson was also trying to understand life, culture and nature, not by the exclusion of such noncommunicative moments, but through them. He told many stories to underline how communication is possible only if nonverbal metacommunication is involved and to what extent it is vital for the existence of life. For example, in his book *Angels Fear* he tells the story of his friend, an anthropologist who studied the congregational life of one community (Bateson 1987: 72-73). Their problems started when the cult plant, one particular species of cacti, which they used in their most sacred rituals, was declared an illegal drug. The church was in crisis as in public opinion this cult became an illegal and morally ambiguous practice. The anthropologist offered his help to resolve the problem. He wanted to make a documentary about the church activities and through filming he wanted to prove that rituals are complex activities and part of the cultural heritage of the group, thus the plant is not just an ordinary drug. The elders were contemplating the opportunity, but after heated discussions decided to avoid the filming and documentary. The dilemma was to choose between the integrity of the cult (and not let outsiders see secret rituals and make these rituals documented and explicit) and its survival (proof that it is not a form of drug abuse). The elders eventually decided that integrity was more important, for even if they managed to maintain the legal status of their church, after their most sacred rituals went public this church wouldn't be the same anymore.

In our research we also often faced the same dilemma of disturbing integrity versus chasing survival. It was not about the legality of the things our informants were doing to maintain their traditional lifestyles (though sometimes this was also an issue). Here we were always feeling that after we put the descriptions of these lifestyles into words and texts, they sounded either too exotic, or too banal. They were losing their liveliness and exciting immersive effect. Verbal explanations of why people were doing things their own particular way very often sounded fake to us. It was as if during these silent moments of collective fatigue in a hut at night, they would start to tell us some old Evenki folk tale recorded in the beginning of the nineteenth century by Russian folklorists and then rewritten by the younger generation of Soviet researchers to be more connected to Marxist ideology, and then finally printed in the school books of Evenki children, who learnt these stories in boarding schools while obliged to spend most of their youth in the village separated from their parents and grandparents. We as anthropologists in this case would once again play the roles of those who help to register cultural artefacts and support claims for their survival, but whose work would unintentionally destroy the culture's integrity. We did not want to take this step, and thus were constantly struggling with our own discipline's obsession with documenting culture and turning it into a testament of itself.

The challenge was how to understand life in a particular place without creating unwanted evidence and a potentially rigid narrative that points out some things, discriminates against others and creates a story that can be used to teach others how to be Evenki. What we wanted is to turn these moments of sincere silence into our sources of information about Evenki lifestyles. Those who would read our book would need to experience silent reading, which is reading not a narrative, but reading a tacit message sent through colours, shades, shapes, swift lines and images. It was obvious that visual images would be the primary medium here. But we needed to develop a strategy to prevent our images from forming a narrative. Our ethnographic materials should avoid storytelling, there should be no protagonist, such as a hunter, or any person, there should be no introductory or concluding thoughts. We needed a methodology that would help us make our ethnographic evidence useless in terms of their conversion into an encyclopaedic article about Evenki culture, or the Russian periphery. The aim of this book is not to tell our readers how modern Evenki people live, the aim is to make our readers recognize many miniature details about Evenki lifestyle by themselves, immerse themselves into the flow of daily routines, and feel these moments of silence, when without words you simultaneously see how you are sitting in this small hut in the forest and also in a huge universe with stars around you.

The microcosms' title of our book refers to this attempt to explain why people do certain things not through references to their motivations, customs, market logics or other stories that would make them protagonists of narratives written by somebody else. Here we can cite Bateson again:

> "In sum, the inner functional topology of the circuits which determine behaviour comes to be a reflexion of, or a microcosmic diagram of, the total matrix, nature, in which the microcosm is embedded and of which it is a part. It used to be said that the organism, Man, was created in the image of God. And it was perhaps an error to reverse this statement and say that Man created God in his own image. It looks as if, in truth, every organism is of necessity created in the image of nature, or should we say creates itself in an image of nature under her strict jurisdiction." (Bateson 1991: 104)

There is a misconception that "microcosm" is referring to some closed and separated system, this is exactly what the term "microcosm" is not about. On the contrary, "microcosm" is a system that is in constant relation and open to other systems, but what is more important, it is not just a hologram or a miniature universe.

"Microcosm" is a metaphor that helps us to show that the Evenki world is not a closed and fully equipped culture that we can describe through inventorying all its knowledge, practices, skills or storylines. Just the opposite, the Evenki world is porous and ever changing, but certain processes that make this culture *look* stable, unique and different are actually processes that are not unique to it at all. Again, following Bateson here: "What if "Truth" in some very large and, for us, overriding sense is information not about *what* we perceive (the green leaves, the stones, that voice, that face) but about the *process* of perception?" (Bateson 1991: 227). So instead of describing how Evenki people struggle and deal with economic disadvantages or the ecological degradation that threatens their lifestyles (both questions are important, but avoided in this book), we show here how their lifestyles are connected to global economic forces, ecological environments, technological progress and finally the universe. We are not saying what happens to Evenki, or what they do, we show how the worlds of the Evenki and worlds of other kinds are mixed and interact, which leads to the possibility (becoming as it is often said) for Evenki to suffer from the economic processes of the global market, technological transformations and ecological catastrophe.

To some extent our description looks as if it's lacking events, it is not dynamic, these are not stories, these are snapshots of the moments when something is happening. And looking at the snapshot you cannot say what is happening, but you can feel what everybody captured in the snapshot feels and in what relations they are. Snapshots like screenshots help to avoid prioritizing movement, you do not ascribe agency only to those objects that move, instead, you can see in detail how things we would never have time to recognize in life and in movies play important roles in events and change realities. So instead of writing notes and providing descriptions, we were using cameras to take numerous snapshots of events in the field. This let us reinvent an old and unfairly forgotten research method proposed by Margaret Mead and Gregory Bateson long ago, a photographic analysis.

In 1942 the world anthropological community was provided with one of the most outstanding results of anthropological fieldwork – the book presented by well-known anthropologists Gregory Bateson and Margaret Mead about Balinese character (Bateson – Mead 1942). The book contained 100 charts and more than 700 photos selected from 25,000 Leica negatives made in the course of their collaborative fieldwork in Bali. Photos played the main role in the book and were organized according to categories, which anthropologists elaborated on during the coding and analysis of their visual data and ethnographic field notes. The book became a classic handbook for visual anthropologists (such as Pink 2007), but also raised reflexive feedback both from anthropologists (Grimshaw 2001) and researchers from other social sciences (Silverman 1993). The attempt was a success according to most reviewers and was then repeated by Mead in collaboration with Macgregor (Mead and Macgregor 1951), although this was more an illustrative work in which the authors described the pre-existing categories that were used in psychological theory with photos taken by Bateson. Later, Gordon Jensen and Luh Ketut Suryani repeated the project, retaining the structure of the book that Mead and Bateson used in 1942, but they used other categories and even tried to re-examine and criticize the earlier interpretation of Balinese culture (Jensen and Suryani 1991).

Critical and supportive discussions very often are prompted by materials collected from fieldwork in the same areas where the authors of classical manuscripts worked. The most famous examples include the refutation of Mead's work on Samoa (Mead 1928) by Derek Freeman (Freeman 1983) and a less scandalous study of Naven rituals among the Iatmul, conducted by Michael Houseman and Carlo Severi (Houseman and Severi 1998) after Bateson (Bateson 1958 [1936]). Attempts to conduct similar research with explicit associations in methodology and theoretical background, but in other areas, are much rarer. In our research, we have conducted photographic analysis according to the logic and scheme employed by Bateson and Mead in 1942, but based on materials collected in the present day among Evenki people, modern hunter gatherers living in Siberia. The research methodology proposed by Mead and Bateson seems to be very effective for the study of the Evenki because it provides the opportunity to include nonverbal elements basic to this egalitarian society, both at the stage of analysis and in the presentation of the results.

From September 2008 to November 2009, we worked among Evenki people at three different field sites in Baunt in East Buriatia. We spent the autumn of 2008 and the first half of that winter in the Evenki village of Ust'-Jilinda. In the middle of the winter, we moved to Ilakachon and stayed there until the spring to study the life of an isolated reindeer-herding Evenki community. During the following summer and autumn, we moved to another Evenki group living near the Taloi and Kudur rivers. These Evenki people were maintaining contact with jade miners for the majority of the year. István Sántha had visited this region and conducted two months of fieldwork there for the first time in 2004. When we started our fieldwork, the aim was to write a book about the situated non-verbal aspects of Evenki culture, which would be based on an analysis of video and photographic materials. Tatiana Safonova worked with a simple Konica Minolta DiMAGE 23 digital camera in the autumn of 2008 and the spring of 2009. Then she changed to a Pentax K1 mirror reflex camera, equipped with a normal 2/35 millimetre Pentax digital objective. She shot black and white photos with the Konica-

Minolta and then made color pictures with the Pentax. István worked with a Nikon-FM2a, using a normal 1.4/50 millimetre Nikkor manual objective and Kodak Elitechrome slide-positives. Tania mostly shot photos around campsites while István Sántha worked more in the taiga. Altogether, we took around 14,000 negatives and 3,000 slides, respectively, during this period. Besides taking photos, we also wrote diaries and created videos (almost 100 hours in total). We tried to shoot photos randomly in order to collect a wide spectrum of materials not restricted by strong preconceptions, and so as to analyze them afterwards, providing a chance to recognize things that were not noticed in the field.

The book contains six chapters which cover various aspects of life in the taiga, from shamanic rituals to the jade trade. Each chapter was structured according to a similar procedure. After we downloaded all photos into one catalogue, we started to tag them with codes. First these were codes of simple objects and actions depicted in the images, such as dogs, huts or drinking tea. Then when we looked through photos with the same tags we realized that they also could be coded in a more detailed way, like 'drinking tea in the forest' and drinking tea inside the hut', thus we added new tags such as outside and inside, and added these tags to photos originally not involved in subcategories, such as "drinking tea". Our analysis followed this zig zag logic of movement between more abstract and more concrete codes. At some point these movements led us to particularly informative photos that included comparatively more codes than others. This is how we chose our starting plates, showing the introductory images representing certain topics such as hunting or reindeer herding in the chapters. Honestly speaking, the coding process took a lot of time, and was mostly dull and boring. But from time to time, these movements between scales, topics, tags and photos brought up unexpected ideas and observations that suddenly explained massive relationships between tags and images, which we hadn't previously recognized, but had held as mere coincidences.

The first chapter is devoted to shamanism, but because our approach is neither narrative nor humancentric, shamanism in our interpretation becomes a 'microcosmic diagram' following Bateson's terms, which helps to organize things and processes in everyday life. Starting with a shaman tree we show how the Evenki microcosm is related to the macrocosm in the same way fractals are related to each other. A shaman tree is not only an ensemble of things, it is a living system, which repeats the same patterns of organization as other microcosmic entities, such as a hunting hut or a hunter himself.

The second chapter on hunting describes hunting as a circuited process, which over and over again goes through phases of anxiety, excitement, joy and calm. What is most interesting is that our analysis has shown that these emotions are symptomatic states of humans, and that all other counteragents involved in the process, both animate and inanimate, pass through the same cycle and have the same kinds of emotions, or better, affects. But these affective circles between people and other agents, such as dogs, guns or fur, are never synchronized, so, for example, when people experience anxiety, their dogs go through a phase of joy.

The following chapter is about gathering, a topic which is rarely covered by anthropologists of Arctic and Siberian people, due to the contrasting excitement and popularity of hunting as a research topic. Meanwhile gathering is a central and an epistemological activity, and it includes not only gathering berries and firewood, but also structurally refers to packing things, collecting amulets or making order out of a mess. Gathering is thus not just an economic activity, it is a way of getting information about the world and a way to deal with its entropy. Through gathering, people break chaos into segments and organize their environments into ordered settings.

In the chapter about reindeer herding we start with an observation, that people love to just watch reindeer herds. We show how the herd is sensitive to the environment it moves through and how through the organization and behaviour of the herd, people connect to the environment and its natural processes. The emotional support that the herd is providing to people living in the taiga is also an important matter, and through snapshots we show how this is connected to the aesthetic appeal of the herd. The latter is an explication of the way the herd is collecting information about the environment and transmits it through its movements and interactions. The beauty of the herd is an encoded beauty of the taiga in which it lives.

The next chapter is devoted to the way technologies are used in everyday Evenki life. Although the titles of the previous chapters can provide a false image that the Evenki are an unspoiled shamanic tribe that still survives through hunting, gathering and reindeer herding, the content of all chapters shows that these practices include technologies from different times, from very old to exceptionally new and experimental. In this chapter we show how new technologies are integrated into taiga lifestyles. On the one hand all new technologies that make life more comfortable and effective are very welcome. But there is one important condition - only those technologies that have old-time back-up technologies remain a part of everyday life. For example, chain saws are extremely popular, but their use means that simple hand saws also stay in the households, because at any moment the fuel can run out or the chain saw can break, so there needs to be an old unbreakable although less effective analogy that would help to prepare firewood. Thus, the implementation of new technologies simultaneously strengthens the roles and positions of old ones. Evenki lifestyles are preserved with the help of new technologies, not endangered.

The last chapter describes how the Evenki organized jade extraction and trade. Here we aimed to show how jade was transported through old Evenki territories from the quarry in the middle of the taiga to the central warehouses. We show that jade was sent as a pulsating signal that went through a channel built up on the territories, where Evenki knowledge, experience and lifestyle were essential infrastructure to maintain it. We show that the Evenki lifestyle is not exclusively based on traditional occupations but can embrace industrial production. And traits of these industrial occupations are encoded into the taiga that surrounds Evenki people.

Bibliography

Bateson, Gregory 1958 [1936]. *Naven: A Survey of the Problems Suggested by a Composite Picture of the Culture of a New Guinea Tribe Drawn from Three Points of View*. Stanford, Calif.: Stanford University Press.

Bateson, Gregory 1979. *Mind and Nature: A Necessary Unity*. New York: E. P. Dutton.

Bateson, Gregory 1987. *Angels Fear: Towards an Epistemology of the Sacred*. New York: Macmillan.

Bateson, Gregory 1991. *A Sacred Unity: Further Steps to an Ecology of Mind*. 1st ed. New York: Cornelia & Michael Bessie Book

Bateson, Gregory, and Margaret Mead 1942. *Balinese Character: A Photographic Analysis*. New York: The New York Academy of Sciences.

Freeman, Derek 1983. *Margaret Mead and Samoa: The Making and Unmaking of an Anthropological Myth*. Cambridge, Mass.: Harvard University Press.

Grimshaw, Anna 2001. *The Ethnographer's Eye: Ways of Seeing in Modern Anthropology*. Cambridge, UK, and New York: Cambridge University Press.

Houseman, Michael, and Carlo Severi 1998. *Naven, or the Other Self. A Relational Approach to Ritual Action*. Leiden, Boston, and Köln: Brill.

Jacknis, Ira 1988. Margaret Mead and Gregory Bateson in Bali: Their Use of Photography and Film. *Cultural Anthropology* 3(2): 160–177.

Jensen, Gordon D., and Luh Ketut Suryani 1992. *The Balinese People: A Reinvestigation of Character*. Singapore and New York: Oxford University Press.

Mead, Margaret 1928. *Coming of Age in Samoa*. New York: Harper Collins.

Mead, Margaret, and Frances C. Macgregor 1951. *Growth and Culture: A Photographic Study of Balinese Childhood*. New York: Putnam.

Pink, Sarah 2007. *Doing Visual Ethnography: Images, Media and Representation in Research*. London and Thousand Oaks, Calif.: Sage.

Silverman, David 1993. *Interpreting Qualitative Data. Methods for Analysing Talk, Text and Interaction*. London and Thousand Oaks, Calif.: Sage.

Acknowledgements

This book is the result of a life-long project. It started with a fascination with Bateson and Mead's work. The fieldwork was an expensive endeavour and we conducted it with support from the Wenner-Gren Foundation (International Collaborative Research Grant 2008) and a Keizo Obuchi fellowship (2008 UNESCO). The phase of analysis and writing up took many years, and we are grateful for this possibility to the Institute of Ethnology, Hungarian Academy of Sciences where this project was conducted as part of a Mobilitas Programme (2011-13 European Union – Hungary NKTH-OTKA). First results were published and presented at many research institutions, and the final publication of this book became possible thanks to the Russian Foundation for Basic Research (RFBR, research project 18-59-23007). We are forever indebted to our Evenki hosts, who took care of us in the field. Our texts were edited by close friends and important people, who not only corrected our mistakes, but also asked tricky questions and left critical remarks. Among them are Dominic Martin, who made an enormous contribution, Tristam Barrett and Ádám Molnár. Our special thanks go to Ivan Golovnev and Elena Golovneva, our collaborators in a project devoted to the history and development of visual methods in the anthropology of Siberia and the Russian Far East.

1

2

3

4

5

6

7

1. The Shaman Tree I

The shaman tree is an ordinary young cedar that grows five minutes walk from the winter hut. Several small sacks and ribbons hang on its branches. There is also a small table attached to it. The small sacks are made of plastic waterproof tea bags and contain various kinds of things, such as tea, sugar, cigarettes, and boxes with matches. Small pieces of bread also hang on the cedar's trunk. As we have observed, these were not untouchable things, but a kind of storage in case of emergency. All the things collected on this tree are devoted to spirits and are essential in hunting—they are the provisions that a hunter takes with him when he sets off into the taiga to hunt. The shaman tree is not an untouchable construction, but alive, a young tree that grows, with things that are valuable not because of their market price but due to their roles in hunting. When people get new provisions they take pieces of these and hang them in sacks on the tree. When there are unlucky times of hunger or deficiency, they take these things from the tree for their own consumption. As a result, the life of a shaman tree is not a representation of an ideal ever- affluent state, but correlates with the life of people, with its ups and downs.

1 The shaman tree with a little table, small sacks, and ribbons. The sacks are made of plastic, are waterproof, and preserve their contents from humidity. They contain sugar, cigarettes, matches, tea, and flour.

2 Rita came to the tree when we were out of cigarettes and other important provisions. While searching for the sacks with cigarettes she was also holding an unleavened cake, cooked with leftover flour. She brought this cake and hung it on the tree. At the time we were starving, waiting every day for provisions that would be brought to the camp by relatives.

3 Rita was very happy to finally find the sack with cigarettes. She remembered that there were two such sacks, and opened the second sack also.

4 The sacks are tied up with ribbons exactly like those that are simply hanging on the branches of the tree.

5 Rita took out the cigarette packs, opened them and took out one cigarette. She put this cigarette back into the sack so that it was not left completely empty.

6 She then tied the sack back in the tree. It was not important to place it exactly where it had hung previously.

7 After that, Rita put things—such as a small cup—that were on the small table in order and left the place with the cigarettes. During this episode she did not say any special spells, but talked about their circumstances when they had tied things up on a previous visit to the tree. She was in a good mood and did not complain about the situation that made her take cigarettes from the tree. Basically she acted like a forager who had found something and felt happy about it.

1

2

3

4

5

6

2. The Shaman Tree II

The shaman tree makes connections between times of plenty and times of shortage. From this perspective it is a kind of time machine, which helps people to come back to the moments when provisions are plentiful, when in reality they are short of them. They not only can collect small portions of the things that are important for hunting, but they are also given a reminder of the circularity of life's processes. They remember how lucky they were when they hung those objects on the tree. And when their luck returns, people remember the hard times, come back to the tree, and hang the spirits' share of their provisions on its branches. The sacredness of the objects is not in their material or form, or in the narratives attached to them, but in the part they play in the reversible flow of things in the environment. People come back to the tree, bring things to it, and take things from it. This is a ritual practice, as well as being very routine and pragmatic. In this way this practice and the shaman tree itself are expressions of Evenki shamanism, and we can think of the shaman tree as a scheme of a shamanic ritual.

1 When we finally received provisioning, Rita went back to the tree with a slice of freshly baked bread and a pack of cigarettes.

2 She put the slice of bread on the trunk of the tree.

3 Rita untied the sack in which a single cigarette had been left.

4 She put the new pack of cigarettes into the sack and tied it back on the tree.

5 The new things that she brought were of better quality, both the bread and cigarettes. On the tree they were mixed with old things without any obvious order or privileged position.

6 After this she left. On this occasion the mood was slightly different, there were fewer jokes and more tranquility, although the context of the situation was much happier than on the previous visit.

1

2

3

4

5

6

7

8

3. The Table

The table is a common detail of a comfortable environment—people stand and sit around tables producing and consuming things, just talking with each other, or resting. The table is a stage for sharing: you can put things out for everyone present around on the table. The sharing of food is parallel with the sharing of ideas, opinions, and information, all of which happens at the table. The egalitarian ethos of hunters, whereby almost everything is shared, is materialized in the form of the table. The table is not a symbol of the hunting ethos, but a pragmatic extension of it. At the shaman tree people need a table on which to assemble items of food and cups with drinks to share not only with spirits, but with their own selves when caught in an emergency.

1 A small table is nailed to the trunk of the shaman tree. The several small plastic cups standing on the table are occasionally filled with vodka. Alcohol evaporates and is never stored at the shaman tree in other ways, mainly because it is a product that cannot be stored at all and should be consumed as soon as a bottle is opened. Vodka is never a part of the hunting provisions; it is the essence of sharing, something that cannot be stored for a moment but should be shared and collectively consumed immediately.

2 Tables are not exclusively used for sharing—sometimes types of tables are built in the forest to store meat and keep it from wolves and other animals. But meat cannot be kept like this for a long time. Such tables are used only if a hunter has man- aged to kill more than he can bring home, so he stores the meat so that he can return and collect it later.

3 Drinking and having a party are unimaginable without a table around which people can sit drinking and talking with each other. A winter camp house also has such a table at which occasional guests who bring alcohol are welcomed.

4 Soup is the predominant dish at everyday meals, as are also warm tea with sugar and bread—which are accepted as a dish on their own. Poverty dictates the domination of dishes that are warm and liquid, rather than rich in calories and concentrated. During times when it is more difficult to store food, both soup and tea tend to become more watery and hot. Without a table it is almost impossible to consume such hot and liquid meals.

5 The table is a workbench at which people do not just eat and cook, but where they clean and calibrate their guns, carved wooden things, sew and make other repairs. Usually there is one table that has such multifunctional usage.

6 In the evening an oil lamp is the only light in the house and the table becomes a center of the hunting hut, like a fire for those who sleep in the forest during hunting trips.

7 The ponyaga—a wooden plate that hunters carry on their backs, to which they bind sacks with provisions or meat—is also used as a mobile table in the forest.

8 The table of the administrator is a new thing in the life of the Evenki. Ira is the only Evenki woman who works in the local village administration. Most of her duties are also connected with sharing and distribution. She helps other Evenki to collect the documents they need to claim state allowances for disability or in case of the loss of a family's breadwinner, paid to a single mother or pensioner.

1

2

3

4

5

6

7

8

9

4. Bread

All the products that are carried into the taiga and are used as provisions for hunting (and hanging on the shaman tree) are not only nutritious but also help to establish relationships with animals and are essential for relaxation. Bread is one of the most obvious examples of a kind of reinforcement, which people consume themselves and share with their animal partners. Like other provisions, flour has a strange origin in the hunting context. To obtain flour, hunters have to earn money (whether through hunting or through other jobs or allowances) and to integrate into the wider context of a market economy. Hunting consists of periods of isolation, but it is always dependent on supplies from the outside world. The shaman tree with its items of hunting provisions is a display of the rate of interaction with strangers. For example, bread is baked differently when flour is plentiful—which indicates that interaction with the outside world is intensive—than when people are short of it due to their exclusion from exchanges with other people. Pieces of bread that have been baked in the oven hanging on the tree are a sign of the former, and a little cake prepared in the pan reflects the latter situation.

1 When flour is plentiful, it is important to save it from frosts and humidity. Even in the house, appropriate conditions for storage cannot be guaranteed, so large amounts of flour tend not to be stored. This predetermines the occasional periods of a deficit of flour.

2 Baking bread in the oven is possible only when flour is in excess, and an excess of flour usually results in the production of an excessive number of loaves. Making yeasty dough and preparing an oven take the same amount of time and effort whether three loaves are baked or ten. Consequently, people tend to bake more loaves at one time, eat more bread, and exhaust their flour supply faster.

3 When there is less flour, people start to bake unleavened cakes with soda. These cakes are cooked in pans. When in the taiga people usually bake such cakes, but in the village they are rarely made. The cakes are called orochonskie lepëshki and are associated with traditional Evenki food.

4 In villages you can find not only home-baked bread on the table, but also fancy cakes bought in shops. This luxury is mostly bought for children. But baking bread at home is still the main trait of an Evenki household, even in the village.

5 Thin slices of bread covered with jam made from forest berries are the most widely spread and popular refreshment, and are usually consumed with hot sweet tea. People of all ages and genders seem to like this repast.

6 Bread with tea constitutes a basic part of every meal taken in the forest. When people go for a week or longer and know that they will be staying in distant hunting huts, they take flour and bake unleavened cakes. But for meals eaten by a fire in the open air bread is the optimal form of food.

7 Bread is one of the main types of provision taken into the forest.

8 Little pieces of sweet crusts of bread are given to the dogs after a successful hunt for sable to calm them down. Bread is a substitute for wild meat.

9 Bread is also shared with reindeer. In practice, salt and bread are the main forms of inducement to make reindeer return home from the taiga. Even when there is not enough for people, small pieces of bread are given to the reindeer.

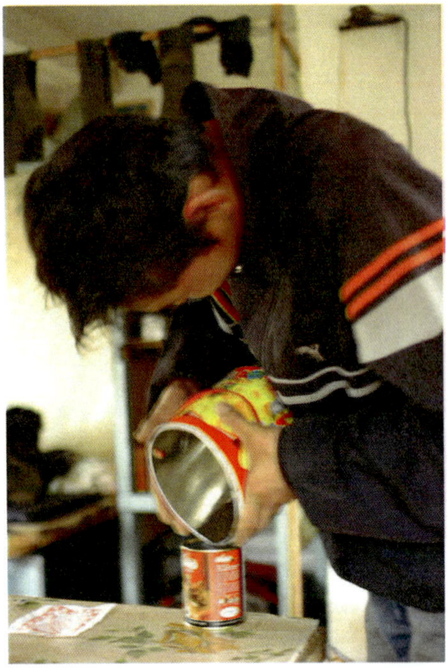
1

2

3

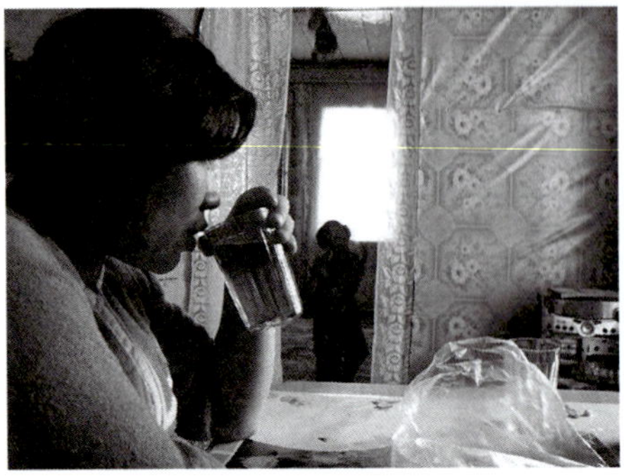
4

5

6

7

8

5. Tea

Tea makes people feel fresh and active. It also cures flu, warms, and calms, as required. People begin every day by boiling water and preparing fresh tea, the first drops of which they share with the fire in the oven and sprinkle in the direction of the sun and the other corners of the earth. These drops are devoted to the spirits to bring luck. The way people drink tea is very individual, as everyone has his or her preferences whether to add sugar and milk, or to drink it hot or cold. Drinking tea together is common and the most basic collective action, but this practice also leaves space for personal experiences, as holding a cup and drinking provides a moment for concentration on your personal feelings, thoughts, and experiences. When people drink tea they rest. Drinking tea constructs a point, which helps to start new circles of activities and projects. This moment of calm and slow movements, when people warm them- selves and relax, is also a moment of communication, when ideas and emotions can be shared with others. Like other provisions that are important in hunting, tea as a substance helps to mark certain points in the flow of actions which can be used as points for synchronization of the actions of different people and creatures. At these moments, when people rest, they share what they have experienced and establish relationships with others (companions, dogs, prey, spirits, and so on).

1 Hunters bring tea into the forest. Their trips are punctuated by rest stops for tea. Such a rhythm is physically and psychologically important for them if they are to stay healthy in an environment full of emergency and unpredictability.

2 Drinking warm tea in the forest is important not only in winter, but all year around. Every time fresh tea is made on the fire the first drops are sparkled into the fire. This action is so common and so much part of a routine that people do not reflect on it and do it almost automatically.

3 When people drink tea they do not need to keep eye contact with each other; they are assembled not for a ritual or in response to an order, but by the opportunity to have a warm drink. Warm tea is the focus of the gathering, and people have to coordinate their actions not with each other, but with the temperature of the drink. Drinking tea provides a focal and external point for the collective actions of people, who coordinate their actions without verbal direction.

4 Poverty is obviously reflected through the cup of tea. Weak tea, not colored with milk and without sugar, may be the only entertainment during times when supplies are scarce.

5 In times of plenty everybody gets the chance to enjoy tea according to their own taste, with three or even more spoons of sugar or with canned cream. Abundance leads to individuation, and scarcity is associated with unification.

6 Individuals who have experienced life in jail sometimes continue to drink a very strong brew of tea, which has a mild narcotic effect.

7 Morning starts with fresh tea and the tea offering, which is done almost mechanically.

8 Sprinkling of tea can be more or less theatrical, depending on the temperament and habits of the person. There is no single rule that says how this should be conducted.

1

2

3

4

5

6

7

8

6. Sweets

Sweets and sugar are vital products in hunting, because they give energy fast and are easy to carry. Sweets also provide entertainment during long and boring periods of inactivity, when people are waiting for someone to turn up or changes in weather conditions. The addiction to sugar as an easy source of energy manifests itself in various forms. First of all, it is obvious that most Evenki have dental problems. Old people frequently cannot take anything but very sweet tea (with three or even more spoons of sugar per cup), because they simply do not have teeth to chew the meat that they may get through hunting. The dependence on alcohol in adulthood has its prototype in childhood. Children are obsessed with sweets and cannot stop themselves from eating all of them until none are left. In the same way, Evenki adults drink until all the alcohol resources are exhausted. Among these resources is sugar, from which people prepare home brew. The parallels between vodka and sweets can also be followed by looking at patterns of sharing. Alcoholism destroys the Evenki self when the balance between sharing and individual consumption is broken. Just as vodka is an essential vehicle for sharing, so are sweets, which are always shared with animals, spirits, and other people. And such sharing is also a way to establish relationships with others. Thus, sweets, sugar, and alcohol provide not only supplies of energy for hunting activities in harsh circumstances; like all other stimulants, their consumption should be limited, and sharing provides the means to control it.

1 Honey cakes and sweets were the products that Evenki from the reindeer camp regularly ordered and received in enormous amounts. The presence of bowls loaded with sweets on the table was a main sign that provisions were abundant.

2 Old men sometimes cannot eat even bread without moistening it in a cup of sweet tea because they have almost no teeth.

3 Bread with jam is a delicious entertainment, and people eat it with unconcealed pleasure.

4 Drinking home brew made from sugar is the other form of entertainment during melancholic periods. It can lead to unpredictable consequences, such as fights and suicides, which are preferred to boredom.

5 Evenki like to mix various things together, and their tastes can look rather extravagant. Tinned fish with chocolate is a variation of a more traditional combination for Evenki—bear fat with berries.

6 Children cannot be stopped from eating all the sweets at their disposal. Nevertheless, parents never store or hide sweets they have from children.

7 It's not just people who are fond of sweets. Horses, dogs, and reindeer also like them, and people always share sweets with their animals.

8 Sweets and cookies are kept in the box with sacred things. People also throw sweets into the oven or fire when conducting sacrifices.

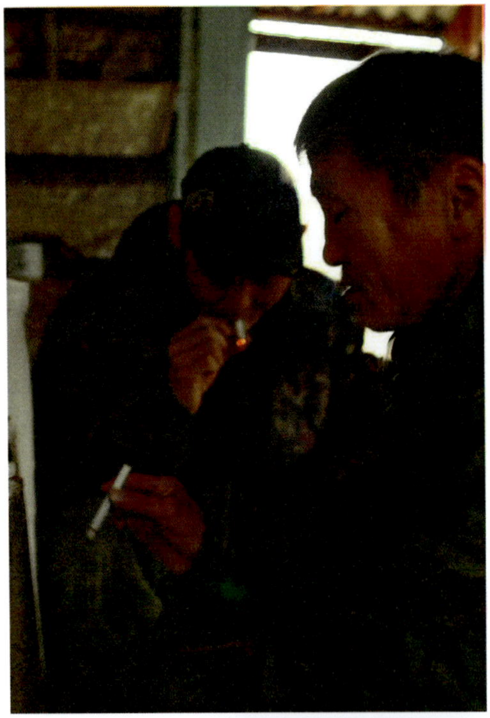

1

2

3

4

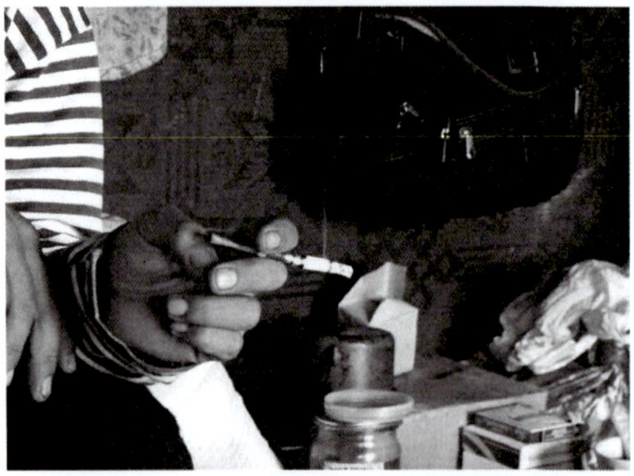

5

6

7

8

9

7. Cigarettes

Nonsmokers are the exception among the Evenki. Most Evenki are very autonomous and independent persons. But most of them need cigarettes, which help them to establish contact with other people and relax with them. Smoking articulates breathing as a form of communication between a person and the world. Breathing not only reveals the emotional state of a person, but through the focus on breathing their state changes. When people smoke together, they synchronize their body rhythms and exchange important emotional messages without verbalizing. Such a form of nonverbal communication is very important in Evenki culture, where there is considerable caution about verbal messages which may be interpreted as a form of demand and spoil egalitarian patterns of interaction. Smoke becomes a kind of medium through which people communicate not only with other people, but also with animals and spirits.

1 Smoking together is an experiencing of co-presence. The exchanging of words is less important than just hearing each other breathing. Eye contact also does not play an important role. People concentrate on their own thoughts and emotions, which are frequently parallel and similar. They do not need to exchange their different perspectives to find a compromise.

2 Frequent smoking of cigarettes is a spontaneous and almost unconscious reaction to any problem or accident.

3 People can smoke doing practically anything, like breathing.

4 What seems disturbing to us is not disturbing for the Evenki. They can talk and smoke at the same time.

5 Cigarette ends are never thrown away but are collected. When cigarettes run out, people start to smoke cigarette end collected before. They even have a special cigarette holder for this purpose.

6 When in a house, people smoke near the oven. The smoke from cigarettes becomes an integral part of the oven fire and its smoke. Through this practice people become connected with the house as a kind of organism.

7 When smoking outside, people often do it around the fire.

8 Smoking stimulates merry moods, jokes, and laughs.

9 Cigarettes are played with and can provoke jokes about smoking itself.

1

2

3

4

5

8. Matches I

Matches are indispensable in the taiga. Usually they are carried together in a kind of set with cigarettes, but of course the sphere of their application is much wider. In an analysis of Evenki shamanic epistemology, matches could be used as a paradigmatic example of a provision that satisfies two needs in the same way as other forms of hunting provisioning—through the initiation of a new circle of activities and communication with other species. These two functions are two sides of the same phenomenon, or two phases of the same circular process. To initiate a new circle of activities an individual (self, body, or system) needs to open itself to the environment and establish a relationship with some outside actor. And, conversely, to enter the communication process an individual needs to initiate a new circle of activities within him/her/itself, so that the interaction will be framed and will be fresh and, at the same time, have a shared context so that it is comprehensive for all the participants. When struck, matches give a distinct visible sign and a point that signifies the start of a new circle of activities. These can be making a fire in the forest or in a stove to prepare food or warm yourself, or lighting a cigarette to smoke on your own or to share with others. And this moment creates a new perspective, when people see their surroundings with new eyes, hear sounds they failed to recognize before, or realize their own pain or tiredness.

1 During hunting people light a match to smoke a cigarette when they are cold, tired, or feel that nothing important is going on. This means that the previous frame of their actions is no longer effective or urgent and they feel they need to change it. This may happen when they have had no luck for some time and are tired of trying to catch sight of an animal or its fresh tracks.

2 The same happens after one has had luck in hunting, when the prey is lying on the ground and the dogs have been tethered to trees so that they cannot steal from the carcasses. The action is over and the hunter needs to switch to new tasks connected with butchering, storing, and transporting the meat.

3 Both lighting a cigarette and making a fire at the site of a kill play the same role of marking a switch of activity, with the initialization of a new cycle of activities.

4 Lighting a fire in the oven is a sign that daytime duties, most of which are conducted outdoors, are over and that from then on people will stay mainly in the house. They will be cooking, eating, and doing small tasks, like repairs and sewing.

5 Sharing a light for cigarettes is a focal point when the two functions of the products that are usually taken into the taiga—tea, bread, cigarettes, sweets, and matches—are most explicitly connected. All these products help people to switch from one particular activity to begin another, as well as to communicate with each other and with other species.

1

2

3

4

5

6

7

9. Matches II

The communication initiated by a sparking match is mediated by smoke. Some species are frightened of smoke; others are attracted by it precisely because of this fear felt by others. Smoke marks territory as a zone of human interference with the prey–predator relationships between various animals and even insects. When people make smoke to connect with spirits they also mark the territory as transformed. Communication with others through smoke is a play with natural hierarchies, a way to reorganize the relationships in ecological settings. At the same time these manipulations are conducted not to control and subordinate other species to their will, but to change the system itself, so as to initiate new circles of communication, action, and experience.

1 A special smudge (fire) is made to protect the horses from insects.

2 Reindeer also gather around smudges. In the morning they set off into the taiga to find moss and grass. When insects become intolerable they come back to the camp.

3 Smudges are also made from old tree stumps that stand in the forest. These smoldering and smoking monuments can be used in various ways, either to frighten and force out wolves from areas where the reindeer are grazing or as a kind of olfactory signpost so that people can find their way back to a place by smelling the smoke from a distance.

4 Making a smudge in the forest is a tricky and special task. The smudge should not be dangerous and should not cause a forest fire. At the same time it should keep smoking for as long as possible.

5 When a sable hides in a den, which can be an extended network of passages between stones or rocks, the hunter makes a fire at the entrance and blows the smoke into the den by flapping his clothes. The dogs are looking on attentively as the panicked sable, attempting to escape the smoke, may appear from anywhere.

6 After a series of hunting failures a gun is cleaned with a special smoke so that it will bring luck.

7 Ribbons are also cleaned by the smoke from a fire before they are tied to tree branches at the sacred place.

1

2

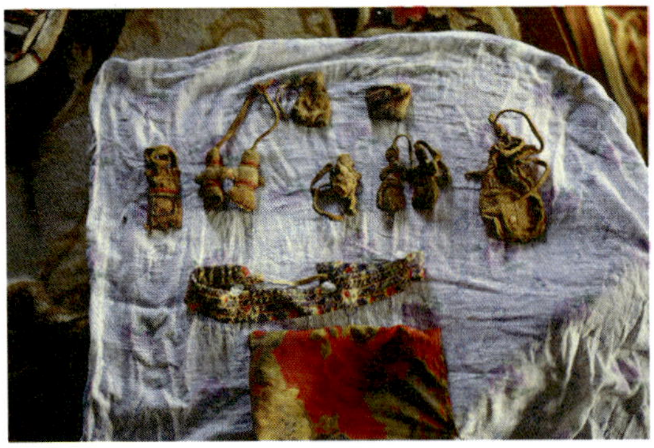
3

4

5

6

7

8

10. The Sack—Contents

The sack is a practical metaphor for the body. Among the sacred things that are kept in a special box are figures of people that also resemble small sacks. In practice, the sack is also associated with the most important aspects of the body: like the body, a sack may be used to contain something fluid, which is stored in it only for some time and not forever; it isolates this content from the outer world, though this isolation is not absolute; sacks are moved around, often being transported from one place to another; and, finally, sacks are tied to other sacks and to people with ropes. The content of sacks can be very different, from flour to soap and nails. But these powders, materials, and objects are never stored in sacks for long—mainly just for the period of transportation. After that things can be kept for some time in the sack, but after a while they are removed, either to be consumed immediately or to be stored in the house, where it is easier to protect them from humidity and freezing. Even when frozen, meat is not stored in a sack because it may become difficult to separate the frozen meat from the sack. Since important things are stored in sacks from time to time, sacks always arouse curiosity. The shape of a sack is never enough to predict accurately what might be in it, just as you can never judge the character of a man by looking at his body. Sacks attract not only curiosity, but also desire. Thus they can be used as an appeal or a lure to attract animals and make them follow you.

1 Mixed fodder for reindeer is one of the only things that is always kept in sacks. But it is consumed so fast that it never is kept for long enough to spoil.

2 Soap is exceptional example of something that may be kept in a sack for a long time.

3 The sacred things of the family included small sack-like figures. These were kept in another small sack, which in turn was hidden in a special bag or box made of birch bark.

4 The preparations for a hunting trip consist mainly of packing up, when various sacks are filled with provisions.

5 After successful hunting, people pack the same sacks with meat that they take to the village to sell things or exchange them for provisions.

6 Vegetables are only kept in sacks when they need to be transported. Usually they are stored under the floor of the house in a special basement. Without ventilation, or unless they are frozen, vegetables rot rapidly.

7 Once we saw how an Evenki carried a cat in a sack when moving from summer to winter camp on horses. The cat was put into a sack whose top was tied and which was then attached to the saddle of a horse.

8 Reindeer follow a man with a sack of mixed fodder. When there is no fodder, reindeer have to be caught and led from the forest to the camp on a rope.

1

2

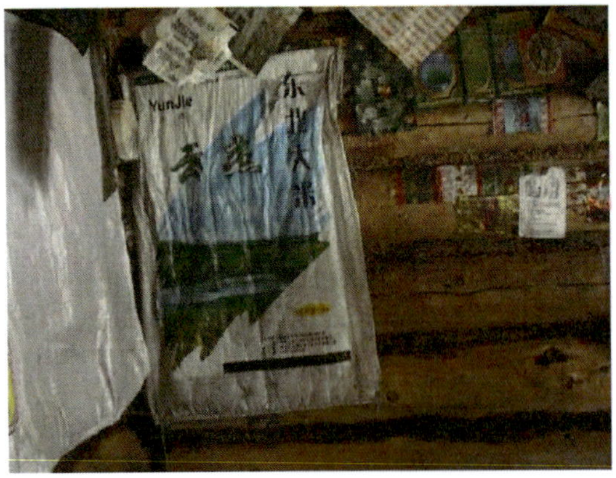
3

4

5

6

7

11. The Sack—Isolation

Isolation is a way to separate things and create a boundary between wet and dry or cold and warm, depending on the purpose of the isolation. Isolation prevents interaction and slows down the processes usually associated with nature. And here we see the problem of the boundary between living and nonliving, which can never be absolutely nontransparent. Likewise, the sack can never guarantee the total isolation of its content from the environment. The act of isolating is a process of keeping a balance between change and conservation. All things are to some extent alive, changing over time because they are influenced by the environment. They absorb water, disintegrate, become rusty, or turn sour. To store and conserve things, one has to destroy the relationships that exist between them and the environment. This can be compared with cutting them out of their context. But this is a process that has several stages. Taken as they are, items like meat or berries will rot when isolated in a sack because they still contain enough water to maintain the process of change. Hence, before putting things into a sack, one has to keep them on the sack so that the water they contain can evaporate. If people want to protect their house—as a kind of body that also needs to be isolated from the outer world—then they have to isolate things brought from outside that have not yet gone through the first stages of isolation.

1 A hunter skins a squirrel on a sack so as not to scatter blood on the wooden floor of the hunting hut.

2 The same precautions are taken when a bird is plucked.

3 People sometimes put sacks on the walls to stop draughts. This is frequently done when hunters have to overnight in hunting huts, when they have the time and the opportunity to renovate and insulate them.

4 After an animal has been killed in the forest, the first butchering is conducted on sacks laid on the ground. This is done to prevent the meat from becoming contaminated by dirt. Such precautions also help to reduce the traces of blood left where the animal was killed that might otherwise attract predators. In winter the use of sacks helps to prevent meat from becoming frozen to the ground.

5 Moss gathered to insulate a new hut is collected in a sack. This lot was stored for some time in the sack, but people worried that it would rot there. So they did their best not to delay the building of a hut so that the effort spent collecting moss would not be wasted. Once begun, the process of insulation needs the attention and actions of people. Otherwise it reverses back, canceling all previous human efforts.

6 Berries are dried and separated from leaves on a sack. The sack is used as a kind of table on which objects are displayed and detached from their previous contexts.

7 From time to time nails and screws are taken out of the boxes or bags in which they are stored to dry and air them, so as to prevent rusting.

1

2

3

4

5

6

12. The Sack—Transportation

The most important function of sacks is their use to transport things and sub- stances. Sacks are suitable for logistics in the taiga because they are neither too rigid nor too loose, so things can be assembled and kept together, but at the same time in a sufficiently flexible state to change shape in response to external pressures. Sacks are moved in a moving environment and are attached to unsteadily moving creatures—people, horses, and reindeer. The flexibility of the sack and the strength of the material from which it is made are its most valued characteristics. But these qualities also need to be constrained, because there is always a possibility that in some circumstances a sack will have to be cut to empty it quickly, get rid of it, or free an animal from it. The same is true of the requirements in respect of the quality of clothes and other covering materials: they should never be so tough that they constrain people in emergency situations. Sacks, people, and animals all move in a moving environment, and so they must also be to some extent open to possible changes.

1 Horses carry quite heavy loads. People sew special sacks to hang on the saddle, and sacks with provisions are put into these saddle sacks. If anything untoward happens, provision sacks are easily removed from the saddle sacks.

2 Reindeer can carry less than horses and their back-sacks are therefore made smaller. Reindeer move more smoothly and, if they bolt, crash with less force into bushes and trees. Their back-sacks are made of leather, not from tarpaulin like those for the horses. They are lighter, more flexible, and give more possibilities to distribute the weight evenly on the back of the animal.

3 To carry provision sacks themselves, people bind them to thin wooden plates, called ponyaga, which are then attached to one's back. Ponyaga can be used as a table on which to cut meat or serve food in the forest. Other important implements, such as axes, are also bound to the ponyaga with ropes.

4 Rucksacks are also widely used. They are preferred when the hunter is accompanied by a horse, because he does not need to carry provisions himself and carries only essentials and other small items in his rucksack.

5 When all-terrain vehicles are used to transport things, sacks are less convenient and boxes are preferred. The luggage module of the vehicle is like a big box, allowing square and rigid forms to be compactly packed. When these vehicles are on the move the ride can be very rough, so anything carried needs to be suitably packed and placed in a strong container, such as a box. Items carried should also be distributed between relatively small units to make loading and unloading easier.

6 Sacks are used when things are transported by car, although in this case they are never attached to each other or to the car, as is usually necessary when horses are used. Here also the processes of loading and unloading are more important than fitting or arranging things inside the vehicle. The car is basically a kind of box that is relatively isolated from the environment.

1

2

3

4

5

6

7

8

9

13. The Sack—Integration

Sacks are connected to other sacks, creatures, bodies, and constructions. Often they are elements of an elaborate system and, as such, they are integrated into these systems. In practical terms, sacks are embodied, which means that they become part of the body of a carrier. The ties that connect a sack to one's body should not be too strong and should provide a flexible bond that can be cut when circumstance dictate. When sacks are assembled around a carrier, the main task is to balance their weights and shapes. The body of the carrier is reshaped as new elements are added. These additions should not prevent the body from moving freely, and this is the most difficult and delicate task to perform. Integration and balance are the two sides of one coin. If the system is imbalanced, it will immediately fall apart. Also, if any part separates, especially when the carrier is on the move, it will become unstable.

1 People never hurry when tying bags and sacks to the ponyaga. This task must be done carefully so that the load won't disturb the hunter when walking. At the same time the hunter should be able to feel the weight so that he can tell if something goes missing.

2 Sacred things are assembled together and represent a complicated system of things that balance and counterpoise each other.

3 The correct distribution of weight on the horse's back is important, because this can prevent injuries and some accidents.

4 Loading a reindeer is an even more difficult task, because reindeer are more delicate than horses.

5 Sacks are often tied to the walls inside and outside the hunting hut. This protects them from animals, humidity, and freezing. The way these sacks are connected with each other and the house can be very complicated.

6 People spend a lot of time on the preparations before a hunting trip. Provisions are graded and distributed between various sacks, which will be connected with each other and loaded on a horse.

7 Small sacks containing poisonous bait are tied to the bone and hung high above the ground on stakes. These constructions are placed in the forest far enough from the camp that the hunting dogs won't scent the bait. The idea is that the bait should attract wolves, which are believed to be more skilled than dogs and able to reach the bait.

8 There is no need to assemble and tie together sacks and boxes transported by vehicles. Instead, these need to be easily separated from each other so that they can be quickly loaded and unloaded. (9) Accidents—when a tied load comes apart—are rare and usually happen with young people who are not experienced enough to assemble things so that different parts balance each other when on the move. Accidents also can happen when the embodiment is not complete, for example the person that leads a caravan does not feel its margins.

1

2

3

4

5

6

7

8

14. Binding the Living to the Living

The small sacks that were hung on the shaman tree were bound to the branches with ropes. When animate and inanimate objects are bound together they constitute one system, which cannot be definitely recognized as fully alive or not alive. Here is the point of transition between life and death. If two living creatures are bound together, their relationship takes the material form of the rope that connects them. The tension that rope experiences is also a tension of interaction, and here we see that social facts have a physical, even mechanical, existence. Abstract thoughts have concrete prototypes in everyday life and do not need special symbols to be grasped and described. When a man takes a dog hunting, he leads her on a rope. At first, when the hunter takes the leash in his hands, the dog is usually very expressive and active. Her excitement may be so strong that it may not be clear whether the dog is attacking the hunter or playing with him. Superficially this might look like a fight, which ends after the relationship between the hunter and the dog settles down and takes a form of subordination, with either the hunter leading the dog, which happens more often, or the dog showing the direction. The same thing happens whenever men take other animals on rope anywhere, although these moments of instability may last only seconds and not be observable. Nonetheless, people are always prepared for them and the possibility that an animal may try to reestablish the form of the relationship. Any external accident can upset the relationship and provoke an animal into revolt.

1 The hunter and his dog feel each other's movements through the tension of the rope and can assess each other's emotional state not only by looking, but also through this constant physical contact.

2 Horses are often hobbled to stop them wandering too far. This does not fix the animal to a certain point but limits its freedom of movement. This is an explicit example of how the redundant relationships within the system—which add no new elements to it—become a burden that makes the system inefficient.

3 It is enough to catch one reindeer and bring it to the camp on a rope to get other reindeer to follow it. When animals notice that one of them is moving steadily in a particular direction, they follow. Having established a relation with one creature, a man can manipulate its behavior and create a pattern for the behavior of others, ultimately con- trolling the whole herd.

4 Sometimes people construct complex systems with several layers, with themselves leading a horse to which a dog is attached on a leash. This makes traveling through the taiga faster, but such a fragile system can come apart any time because of the increased number of couplings.

5 The same is true when reindeer are used for transport, when several animals may be roped in a train.

6 When people stop to have a rest the moment of a possible sudden rebellion comes. The attempts to reestablish the relationship or even to escape it frequently take the form of play.

7 Sometimes it is impossible to identify who is leading whom.

8 Stressful situations, such as vaccination, may provoke animals into showing real resistance. At such times, when it takes several men to drag the creature on a rope, one can see how fragile is human dominance over animals.

1

2

3

4

5

6

7

15. Binding the Living to the Not Living

When people bind or tether animals to other objects, they limit their movements, fix their position in the environment, and make them less active. Binding a living thing to an inanimate object is a kind of deactivation—which could lead to a total blocking that spells death for a living creature. When people bind animals there is always the potential for killing them. In fact, various traps are constructed according to this principle: either they simply immobilize a trapped animal or they throttle it. Therefore, tying an animal to a fence, a post, or a tree is always an act of violence, and animals only accept it with patience or a struggle. The ambivalence of the situation may even be reinforced when people use these moments to pet the tethered animal. In this context it is impossible to distinguish violent and kind actions. They merge and constitute one flow of interaction between an animal and a man. Care and killing become two aspects of one phenomenon.

1 A man tethers a horse to a fence to unload the sacks that it was carrying. This is a transitional moment when the horse is practically unbound from the man to be set free.

2 After a sable has been successfully driven into a tree, the hunter tethers his dogs so that they will not be able to get at its body after it has been shot. The hunter deactivates the dogs because their part in the hunt is over. The dogs likely see this in a different way.

3 When a horse is tethered it is easy to be both tender and violent with it.

4 At camps dogs are usually tied to their owners' huts; here they spend days or maybe even weeks waiting for the opportunity to run free during hunting.

5 Long periods of waiting make dogs more enthusiastic and effective when they finally get the chance to hunt.

6 To prevent reindeer from becoming wild, people bring them into camp from time to time and leave one of the animals tethered so that the others stay around and feel that they are safe.

7 Before being killed, a cow is tied to a fence. Usually very passive and quiet, they can become aggressive and dangerous when they sense what is going to happen.

1

3

2

4

6

5

16. Binding the Not Living to the Living

Because the binding of a living creature to an inanimate object can lead to an irreversible change, such as its death, a mediating move should be made to prevent such a drastic transformation of the system. There is a pattern of action that helps to deactivate deactivation; in other words, if you need to exclude the creature from a system, you bind the living to the nonliving, and if you want to smooth this process, you bind the inanimate object to the living creature. The object is fixed on the body of the animal, or the animal is attached to the external object, not directly, but through a kind of mediating chain. By binding nonliving objects to living creatures, people do not exclude them from the environment but create a potential to include them in their own personal systems of action.

1 Sacks with provisions are never directly bound to horses or reindeer, because they could be dangerous and can injure the animal in emergency situations, when its reactions may be wild and unpredictable. A light saddle is first bound to the reindeer, as well as a collar, which absorb the tension which a rope and a load can cause.

2 A collar on a dog also helps the hunter to control it when he needs to exclude it from the action.

3 A hunter has various useful things, such as gloves, attached to him. This makes them easy to find when needed, and he can forget about them when they are not required. These bound items carry a potential of being used.

4 All horses have collars, which they wear all the time so that they can be caught when needed.

5 Not every reindeer wears a collar and a bell. Only those with a good temper—which are easily caught and which people distinguish from others and like for some reason—wear such collars. Collars and bells are markers that people leave on those animals with which they have most experience and through which they establish relationships with others from the herd. Here we see a chain of markers, which also play the role of mediators, through which various elements of the system connect with each other.

6 Dangerous items like knives, axes, and guns are also attached to the hunter's body using a kind of pocket or sack, although not directly to avoid risk of injury.

1

2

3

4

5

6

7

17. Binding the Not Living to the Not Living

Objects are bound together to be compact, something that is especially important for transportation. Other reasons to bind or attach nonliving objects to other nonliving objects are to store, dry, or process them. In practice, trans- ported things are already in a state in which they can be stored. Binding things together frequently presupposes that they are disintegrated or separated from their previous contexts or systems, of which they were part. When bound to each other, the bond between two or more nonliving objects can always be seen in a context of some active system of things that is assembled around some active, living agent, whether these nonliving things are directly bound to this agent or are marked for potential use. In other words, nonliving things migrate between various living agents, either being bound to them or having a place in the field of the living agents' prospective action. All objects circulate around living creatures, as if drawn by some gravity of life. The little sacks with provisions that are tied to the shaman tree can be seen as such objects that are connected to the living tree, but which from time to time can be transferred into the field of men's actions.

1 The best way to dry and store medicinal herbs is to tie bundles of herbs to the string hanging from the roof of a hut.

2 To butcher a wild roe carcass, men bind its legs and hang it so that it won't get soiled and the ground soiled by blood also will be limited.

3 Poison for wolves is attached to a hut-like construction built in the taiga. It is waiting its time to be involved in the wolf's sphere of action.

4-5 Tree trunks are bound to a tractor or an all-terrain vehicle. Until recently they had to be sawn up into smaller logs to be carried by a reindeer or a man to the camp. Now that new means of transport make it possible to transport huge trunks, the procedure of disintegration is postponed, although at some point logs still have to be cut and chopped. Logs are separated from their previous context and integrated into new systems of action, in which vehicles are merely mediating objects between trees and the people who drive the vehicles.

6 The old way of transporting firewood on sledges conforms to the same pattern.

7 The ribbons that are bound to the branches of sacred trees are in the domain of the spirits. As such they are extensions of these spirits, just as other objects and instruments attached to the hunter are parts of his system of action.

1

2

3

4

5

6

7

18. Hanging Outside

Objects that have been hung outside a house or a hut are in transition—they have neither been stored yet, nor consumed, nor set free. Their status of either being living or nonliving objects is also in question, as hanging is a (sometimes reversible) process of transition from life to death. The most frequent form of suicide among the Evenki is by hanging. Those who feel they lack freedom and mobility may hang themselves outside the house or a bathing house, preferably in the taiga, while those who lack social bonds or a stable point in their lives choose to hang themselves inside buildings. An object hanging outside a house is only temporarily inactive and can be included into a scheme of action on demand. Jokes and play based on the pretense that living things are dead often use hanging as a pattern, or motif, to express this idea.

1 Guns—which are usually hung outside houses and huts—are always loaded and ready to fire. This is especially important in the taiga, where wild animals such as reindeer or bear can intrude at any moment, so one always needs to be ready to defend oneself. This practice is often dangerous for people too, because if anyone loses their temper (for example during drinking) loaded guns kept outside the house can be used at once, giving no time for thought or discussion.

2 The food in the sack that has been hung on the top of this hut-like construction is there to be kept out of the reach of the hunting dogs. In fact this rarely helps because such a form of temporary storage provokes the dogs even more, as the wind spreads the smell of food. When poisoned meat is hung in the forest for wolves, its smell spreads over a much larger area than when something is stored on the ground, and hence it attracts predators.

3 The bowl with water suspended over a fire in the forest is part of a living system, the creation of which and interaction with which are essential to the hunter if he or she is to stay alive.

4 The carcass of a still warm animal hangs in the yard. It is being butchered quickly because this is possible only when it is fresh, not frozen, the muscles have not yet hardened, and the blood has not coagulated. Some basic characteristics of a living body— warmth and flexibility—are still present.

5 Hanging is a predominant principle used with various traps, because animals that are caught should not be killed immediately; if they are, their bodies will freeze and it will not be possible to skin them. Trapped animals, usually sable or hares, hang half alive, sometimes unconscious, waiting to be collected by a hunter.

6 Cats, because of their similarities in size and constitution with sable, are commonly the object of jokes.

7 Children also play with the idea of being hung and swaying in the wind, like the sacred things that hang on sacred trees.

1

2

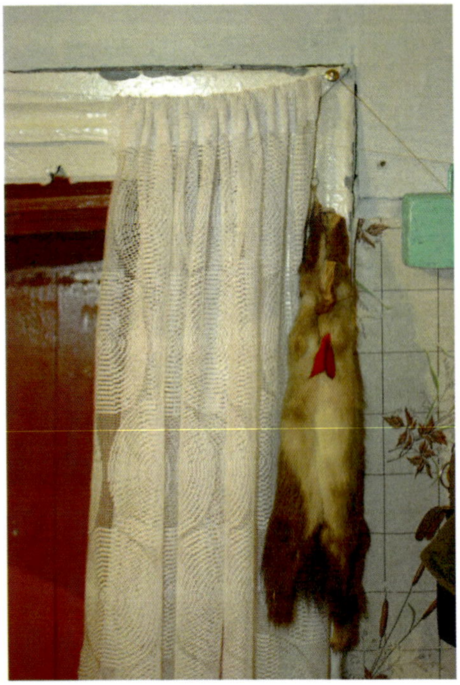
3

4

5

6

7

8

19. Hanging Inside

Objects that are temporarily or permanently hung inside the house are parts of the internal order in the organization of various things. Those things that are left hanging for a long time tend to be associated with the house itself and add something to the life of the house; examples might be amulets that bring hunting luck, or photo- graphs giving a sense of the presence of those who are far away, traveling, or dead. Other things hang in the house for a more limited time, whether to be kept in sight for some reason or to be dried; in both cases such items are already involved in the system of some projected action, whether they are to undergo further transportation or be stored. When something is hung in the house it is assimilated into the system of the house. It is not only assembled with other hanging things according to the inner logic of the distribution of weights and volumes (the same logic that is behind how sacks are organized on the body of an animal during transportation), but it is also affected by the microclimate of the house with its daily changes in temperature and humidity. At the same time these things themselves add some new character to the atmosphere of the house—for example through their smell. Because objects that are hung in the house are more exposed than if they were stored away, they absorb other smells and water from the air, and as such they also play a role in the regulation of internal climate. The Evenki prefer to hang things rather than put them aside somewhere and isolate them in boxes or cupboards. They have few possessions, and often all that they do have is in use, so they do not need to put them away. At the same time, the limited number of things they have can be easily displayed and organized, as well as readily packed and transported.

1 Sacred things have been hung in the corner in a special box made of birch bark, where they are not totally isolated.

2 During the preparation for a trip important items like a horse bridle are hung for some time inside the house, where they can be dried and kept warm. To accustom a horse to it more quickly, a bridle should be warm and to some extent feel like a living thing.

3 The skin of a rare white sable is the best kind of hunting amulet and is hung near the entrance.

4 The skins of freshly killed sable have been hung out to dry on the walls or under the roof.

5 Photos of loved ones hang on the walls in a display that usually includes both living and dead members of the family.

6 Clothes are normally hung outside to dry even in winter, when they immediately become frozen. People avoid taking wet things inside so as not to increase the humidity of the air in the house. Some food may also be cooked outside for the same reason.

7 Various sacks hanging on the inside and outside walls of the house resemble their mini-versions hanging on the shaman tree not far away in the forest.

8 Large skins are hung outside the house but under the roof. Drying takes more time, but the house is protected from rather special smells associated with such animals as bears.

1

2

3

4

5

6

20. Microcosmos

The traveling man, the hunting hut, and the shaman tree are autonomous units that exist in an environment characterized by movement. They all represent kinds of gravitational centers, with things circulating on the orbits around them. They are also self-regulating, as the movements and positions of the things surrounding them are balanced, or as changes lead to reactive changes in the organization. Things that are essentially provisions are packed into sacks that partially isolate them from the outer world, and these are integrated with each other into a net. Living and nonliving objects are bound together, and these relationships provide a potential for transition and change, when living things become nonliving, and vice versa. Life has its pulse and reaches all the objects involved in the microcosmic system of the man, the house, or the shaman tree.

1 The man on the horse forms a moving, autonomous unit that wends it way through the ever-changing environment.

2 The sacred place with several shaman trees shares many traits with the man and the house. For example, living and nonliving objects are bound to each other.

3 A hunting hut may look nonliving at first sight, but as soon as a fire is lit in the stove and hunting provisions have been hung on the walls a microclimate is formed, affecting and accommodating all the objects together into one system.

4 Some sacred places and shaman trees provoke by passers into certain actions—for example, these ladders have been placed to attract anyone passing by to climb them to take something from the tree or to hang something in the tree themselves. This invitation to contribute to the circulation of life in the system by adding something is a step toward integrating a person and a shaman tree together into the frame of one system of action.

5 The man, his dog, a gun, a sack with provisions—all are integrated into one system. Man and dog can survive and stay alive in the harsh environment of the taiga only by maintaining the integrity of this system.

6 This little house covered with provision sacks and hunting trophies lives its own life, even when people leave it for some time. When a hunter leaves one of his huts in the taiga, he always tries to leave some flour, sugar, cigarettes, and matches. Sometimes he may even leave a bowl with frozen tea, which you can warm and drink with fat when you come from the cold outside into the hut after a day-long trip. Sometimes people return to their huts and collect provisions that they left there, as they do when they go to the shaman tree and take cigarettes when their supply has run out.

1

2

3

4

5

6

7

8

1. The Hunting Cycle

Hunting is a cyclical process that consists of 4 phases that follow each other by turn. These are: the period of absence of meat or fur, when the hunter does not feel sure of whether he (or sometimes she) will find prey in the forest; then the hunter detects the prey, follows, sees or hears it, and is excited in its presence; when the prey is shot and in the hunter's hands, he feels joy; the final phase of hunting is devoted to calmness and ordinary duties, such as the processing of the trophy's carcass or skin, transporting, preparing food and other chores which at some point could be already seen as preparations for a new hunt. These four affective states (anxiety, excitement, joy and calmness) of the hunter are not only expressions of his personal state of mind and involvement in the hunting process, but are also coordination schemes which in different ways involve other participants and agents such as dogs and horses, but also guns, meat and fur. This table depicts a particular hunt, showing all the phases as they followed one another.

1 Vitya went hunting and took his dogs to the taiga. At this moment he did not even know whether they were going for meat or fur.

2 Walking across the taiga and searching for fresh trails took several hours.

3 Finally the dogs bolted and we found them barking and digging at a big tree under the roots of which, we assumed, a sable was hiding. Vitya quickly and enthusiastically joined in digging, trying to get the dogs off, so that they wouldn't catch the sable first. He also tried to cut the roots with an axe.

4 At one point the sable escaped but the only thing it could do was to climb up a tree. That was a trap, because then Vitya could shoot him with his gun. He only needed to tie the dogs to trees, so that they wouldn't destroy the pelt of the sable in their excitement after it fell from the tree top.

5 When the sable fell, shot, to the ground Vitya flashed us a happy smile.

6 Then he showed us with pleasure his trophy, a sable with good quality fur.

7 After this successful shot Vitya collected brushwood and made a fire.

8 He collected snow to make tea and prepare some food. After a small lunch we started home.

1

2

3

4

5

6

2. Phase 1: Anxiety

Hunting starts with the first signs of slight anxiety, when the hunter cannot just concentrate on his everyday chores, but is worried and feels that what he has is not enough (either meat or fur). This anxiety grows and at some point forces the hunter to go into taiga. This first phase is dominated by uncertainty: the hunter does not know whether he will find anything at all. There is no focal point in the surroundings, the hunter scans the scenery and listens to every sound. When he finally identifies sounds, movements or tracks that signal the presence of prey, his anxiety becomes mixed with excitement, which is the predominant emotion of the second phase of hunting.

1 A last cigarette and cup of tea before going off into the taiga. These help to overcome the anxiety, which is at its height, because the hunter does not even know which direction to look for prey.

2 The dogs are very excited and happy, when the hunter takes them with him into the forest. They jump up and down chaotically, and run in various directions.

3 When riding on his horse, the hunter can watch the surroundings from above, which helps, especially in open places. The horse's sounds, its breathing and stepping, need to become an ambient background. The hunter learns not to hear them, just as he learns not to hear the sounds of his own body, the better to notice any movements of other animals.

4 Walking through the taiga is the basic way of searching for prey. At this moment the total body of the hunter is an instrument devoted to detecting prey. Sometimes the hunter does not see or hear prey, but feels its presence, or just feels that something is watching him.

5 Vitya searches for animals through his binoculars. He does not use the telescopic sight attached to his gun for this purpose. The hunter watches with both eyes and gains more information.

6 The hunter hides himself and his dogs and waits for the prey that the other hunter is supposed to chase in his direction. He does not know the exact place where the prey will appear. It is also not clear when it is going to happen or even whether it will happen at all. He can be sitting in a state of such anxiety and readiness for action for a very long time.

1

2

3

4

5

6

3. Phase 2: Excitement

The second phase in hunting is usually rather short, although it can last for several hours in some cases, such as the pursuit of an elk or extracting a sable from its burrow. It starts when the hunter finds the prey, knows exactly where it is and is excited by the possibility of killing it and possessing it. The external focus of attention and interest forms for the hunter a central point in the external world. He tries to follow his target, and with the help of his dogs to fix it in space. When the prey cannot escape; either it is stopped and surrounded by barking dogs, as in case of an elk, or it is forced to be stationary in a tree (if it is a sable), the hunter should seize this moment and shoot. The death of a prey is a moment when the hunter unleashes his concentration and focus on some point in the external world. The intense interaction with the prey, when all the actions of the hunter are coordinated with the prey's behaviour, is over. The excitement is also over, having left the hunter, but not the dogs which still believe that they can get the trophy. The hunter now tries to neutralise his hunting partners, and to isolate the trophy from them and calm them down.

1 The dogs are usually the first to recognize the prey. For a hunter there is a transitional period of time between when he sees his dogs becoming excited, and getting excited himself as he realizes the reason for their emotions.

2 When dogs show the hunter the approximate area in which he ought to find the prey, anxiety is left behind. The hunter does not have any doubts as to whether he will encounter anything; from then on he has a concrete goal, which he needs to mark out from surroundings and shoot.

3 The switch to the phase of excitement can assist the quick performance of difficult tasks in unpleasant circumstances. Here the hunters are trying to drive a sable out of its burrow on a cold winter night, by shifting large boulders in frozen terrain.

4 If it is possible, a hunter prefers to tie up the dogs even before he kills a sable. For example, when the prey is driven from its burrow and climbs up a tree, the hunter takes the time to tie up his excited dogs. The sable won't dare to escape from the tree once the dogs have begun their barking. The excitement of dogs helps the hunter to control the situation and shoot the prey. He knows that he won't accidentally kill the dogs and that they won't destroy the sable's pelt. The phase of excitement is the most dangerous during hunting, especially when man and dog become competitors.

5 Sometimes hunting for squirrels becomes a routine procedure that does not include an intensive excitement phase, partly because the price of a squirrel skin is very low, and partly because hunters can kill more than 20 squirrels a day.

6 However even small prey, such as willow grouse, can provoke considerable excitement, when a hunter kills one after a long phase of anxiety and anticipation. So the intensity of excitement during this phase depends on the context, notably upon the way in which the first phase of hunting has progressed, and the overall experience of the hunter.

1

3

2

4

5

6

7

4. Phase 3: Joy

The third phase of hunting is joyful possession, when the hunter touches and scrutinizes his prey in detail. The weight, texture and quality of fur or meat are experienced through direct contact (a kind of embodiment) which is then followed by detachment, when the hunter first of all shows his prey to others, and then gives it away. For some moments the hunter remains without the prey in his hands, but still experiences joy, which gradually transforms from the joy of possession to the joy of presentation and the joy of being successful. The feeling of success is a moment of change in these forms of joy, when the possession of a concrete object (a catch is held in the hands and is embodied) gives place to the possession of luck (the catch is detached from the hunter's body, but the feeling of joy remains). Showing the prey and giving it to others to hold are ways to experience success, because it is only through detachment of the prey from the hunter's body that the hunter can understand and appreciate its value and not simply experience its qualities. Value is one potential use of prey and the source of the interest of other people in it.

1 When the hunter shoots a squirrel (as with sable), he usually holds it by the tail and shakes it to drain the blood. Most often this is done when walking in such a way that the shaking happens in rhythm with the hunter's steps and motion. The body of the prey is incorporated into the body scheme of the hunter.

2 Birds are usually held by the legs, because in this way the bird's body is less fixed and causes less inertia and resistance, as the hunter walks with it.

3 After skinning, the sable fur has to be dried then washed and dried once again. All these procedures also provide possibility to experience once again the joy of holding it. Processing of the skin provides opportunities to display it and to re-experience the third joyful phase of hunting.

4 The carcass of a wild reindeer is impossible to transport straight to the camp, and the hunter needs to come back several times to the hunting spot, where the animal was killed. Here he constructs a platform on which the meat is assembled after skinning and butchering. This is done to keep the meat from the frozen ground and to prevent wild animals from stealing it. At the same time, the platform creates a visible and distinctive object in the forest environment. After butchering, when the hunter is scented by smells of the flesh, covered with blood and feels the warmth of the newly-killed animal, the meat is laid on platform and hunter can observe it from a distance. It is also presents a suitable background for photographs that aim to document the moment of success.

5 The joy of the moment can be shared with the dogs, who are rewarded with some pieces of meat. The hunters are in merry mood as they make their way back to camp and they frequently play with their dogs then.

6 At various stages of the processing of meat, when some task is completed and the results are displayed, the hunter is given a further opportunity to once again experience the joy.

7 Whenever possible, the hunter delegates the processing of the prey to other people. This helps to separate him from his prey and allows him to experience the wider joys of his success and his luck, rather than just the joy of possession.

1

3

2

4

5

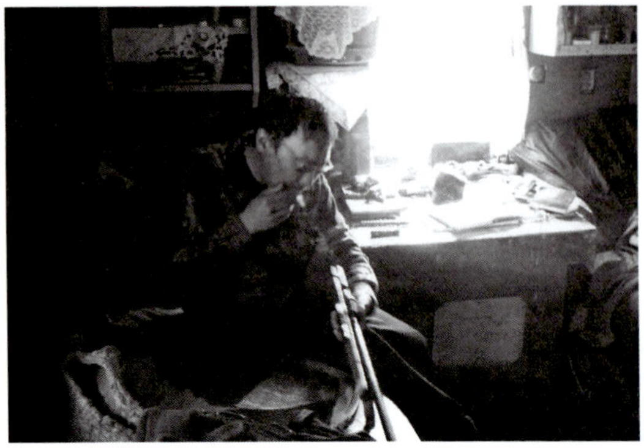
6

7

5. Phase 4: Calmness

The last phase of hunting is devoted to ordinary tasks, during which the hunters either process the products of hunting, or prepare for new hunting cycles. This period is dominated by monotonous tasks, which are slightly joyful in the beginning, because the products of the hunt continue to carry the atmosphere of the previous phase of joy, but as the presence and influence of the products of the hunt starts to wane, the tasks that the hunters undertake become more tedious and boring. When there are no trophies to work upon, such as meat to cook, or sable fur to prepare for sale, everyday tasks do not give satisfaction and relaxation, they are not connected directly with hunting and are not illuminated by it. Cooking after hunting can be compared with a feast, even a small meal at a hunting spot gives high satisfaction and pleasure. But when the meat ingredients obtained in hunting come to end, and meals consist only of staple food, such as rice or potato, cooking itself is seen as boring work. This process comes to a point when anxiety rises and people once again feel the need to go hunting to overcome it. People need to reach the nadir of boredom and anxiety (and sometimes hunger), without which they won't venture back into the taiga for a new hunt. During the sable-hunting season this phase might only take one evening, the length of time which the hunters need to skin sables (and squirrels) caught during the day. In hunting for meat this phase can take somewhat longer, depending on the amounts of meat, the possibilities to preserve it, and number of companions to share.

1 The first butchering of wild reindeer in the forest is hard work but very satisfactory. A display of the amount of meat obtained impresses, especially because usually the hunters go hunting when supplies of meat are totally exhausted. Affluence comes all at once as a big event, whereas the exhaustion of resources (and poverty) is a gradual process and is never experienced as an event.

2 Skinning squirrels should be done in the evening after a day's hunting, otherwise the body of the animal would be frozen and skinning would be impossible. Because squirrels are less valued, this task is experienced as much more boring in comparison to the skinning of sable. Usually a hunter might kill around ten squirrels a day, whereas two sables a day is a particularly successful result.

3 Immediately after killing the hunter makes a fire and cooks tea. This is done because usually the excitement of hunting tempers the onset of tiredness, and the hunter has to prepare hot tea before he feels it. Tasks and chores are interwoven with tiredness and boredom during this phase of calmness.

4 The skinning of sable needs precision and carefulness. If the hunter's shot was accurate, then skinning is easy. But if the hunter has failed to shoot the sable in the eye, then the pelt needs to be sewn to render the damage unnoticeable. Whether shooting or skinning, the hunter needs to perform with accuracy and precision.

5 Cooking fresh meat is a joyful task because it requires less efforts and the meal is tasty. The longer the meat is stored and the best pieces of it are consumed, the more and more elaborated the cooking becomes, with more stages of cleaning and boiling, and the less tasty the meals become..

6 The hunters clean and reassemble guns with patience and accuracy. These tasks are usually experienced as pleasure, and as the hunters carry them out, they anticipate future hunting trips.

7 The more powerful guns need easier care, almost only cleaning and adjustment. But these guns cannot be used in hunting for fur, in which the bullet must not harm the precious pelt.

1

2

3

4

5

6

7

6. The Dogs' Cycle

As companions in hunting, dogs experience the same four phases, but they fill them with their own personal content of emotions and motivations. If, for the hunter, the phases are marked by changes in relations with the prey, for the dogs these phases are demarcated by the hunter, who either lets them run free or keeps them on a leash. Life for a hunting dog is polarised between being free and being leashed, done to make a dog more effective during hunting. The dog is let free usually only in the forest, when the hunter feels that the animal to be pursued is somewhere near at hand (maybe there are fresh tracks or the dogs themselves show that they hear or smell the animal). This is the point when anxiety is changed by excitement for the hunter. When a hunter is shooting, the dogs are always in danger, because they are near the prey. At the highest point of excitement when hunter and dogs are competitors for the prey, sometimes the hunter ties the dogs to trees so as not to let them catch a sable and destroy its fur. When the prey is killed, the dogs always receive something; it could be meat or just a piece of dried bread (in the case of hunting for sable). All dogs have their own inclinations. Some of them are more effective in hunting for meat, others are good at chasing sable. In this respect they are like guns that are different for different hunts. When the hunter chooses which dog to take with him into forest, he also estimates the probabilities of encountering fur or meat preys. Taken home after the hunt, the dogs are tied up in their kennels, where they spend all the time. During these periods of calmness the only events that punctuate their lives are feedings. Immediately after hunting they receive meat or bones, but gradually their food becomes less enticing and they suffer both from boredom and hunger. This makes them active, until they finally are taken once again into the forest to hunt.

1 The hunter sets off into the forest in the middle of the anxiety phase, when he does not know yet whether he will encounter any animal at all. But for the dogs going to the forest is exciting per se, and they experience already what the hunter will feel only when he chases an animal.

2 An especially precious dog is kept on the leash as long as possible, because the hunter is afraid to lose it. If this highly valued dog catches the scent of an animal that is too far away and beyond the reach of a hunter, it is likely to follow it and could be lost in the taiga. Also the dog works better immediately after being unleashed, so this is postponed right up until the moment when prey is spotted.

3 When the sable is chased and driven up into a tree from which it cannot escape, the hunter ties his dogs to nearby trees to prevent them from catching a body of the sable, fallen from a tree after being shot.

4 When the hunter holds the sable skin, he shakes the blood from it, and sometimes lets the dogs lick blood off the skin. This gesture partly compensates for the dogs' exclusion from the joy phase of hunting. This moment is very exciting for the dogs, while for hunter , it is usually performed as a kind of play.

5 Shooting is a crucial moment, when all animals including the dogs are in danger. Accidents happen quite often, mainly because at this moment dogs and people do not coordinate their actions with each other, because both are exclusively attentive only to the movements of the prey. This is a moment, when the dogs and the hunter are competitors.

6 The dogs receive the rewards of their hunting only afterwards when they are fed at home. After a sable hunt they get the whole roasted body of it after skinning, this feast includes the inner organs, blood and bones. The excitement during feeding is comparable to that of going to hunt.

7 During the phase of calmness in the hunting cycle, the dogs are left waiting. They are tied to their cabins and experience a dreadful boredom and sometimes also hunger.

1

2

3

4

5

7

6

8

7. The Horses' Cycle

Horses help people to transport things and to travel during hunting. Most of the time, they are free to graze by themselves. Actual hunting starts when the hunter goes out to capture and tether the horses. First the horses are tied to fences and loaded, then people by turn ride and lead them on reins. Sometimes dogs are tied to the horses during this trip. When the hunter sets the dogs loose, the horses are frequently tied to trees, so that they won't run away when hunter is busy catching prey. The horses are loaded with meat and led back to the camp, and then they are set loose. This is one of the main differences between dogs and horses. For dogs hunting is a short period of freedom and activity, as opposed to an everyday life spent near their kennels in boredom. What is supposed to be accumulated and then performed during hunting is their energy, enthusiasm and activity. Conversely,, horses are harnessed almost only for hunting and it is better if they are calm and passive during these trips. For all the rest of the time they are free. People keep in contact with the horses, provide little portions of delicious food and make smoking fires that protect the horses from insects, but they never fully supply them with hay. Hunters frequently hunt on foot without horses, especially during the sable season. But if they need meat, horses are usually taken, and there are moments when the hunter even shoots sitting astride a horse. This is a particularly dangerous moment, because the horse has to stay calm and not move in the situation, despite the level of extreme excitement. If the horse moves at this moment and the hunter misses, then the horse will be blamed and beaten. Similarly, if a dog barks and frightens the prey, the hunter will beat the dog and can even shoot it in a fit of anger. During shooting, hunters, dogs and horses agitate each other. This is a central moment for the hunting cycle which is characterised by a conflict between all participating agents. Most of emergences associated with hunting happen at this moment, when all participants are in danger of being injured.

1 Catching horses before hunting is the starting point of the cycle, which itself can be seen as hunting in miniature. To find horses the hunter needs experience and intuition, which he needs in the same way to find prey.

2 Oats are the favourite food of the horses, which they cannot resist. The simplest way to calm these semi-wild horses down and straddle them is to pour out oats on the ground.

3 In dangerous places, for example on the icy surface of a frozen marsh, people walk with horses to reduce the risk of injures. For people the capability of transporting things is more important than riding.

4 The decision to let dogs loose and tie horses up in the forest is made after some analysis of tracks. The hunter examines tracks with a special wooden stick, listening to how the snow cracks and testing its freshness. If the tracks seem new, the hunter dismounts from the horse and a new phase of pursuit of a animal starts.

5 The hunter leans on a tree when shooting so as to make steadier, more accurate aiming easier. This would be impossible to do sitting on horse's back.

6 After the shot, the skinning and the initial butchering, meat is transported to the camp. This is practically the main reason, why horses are needed for hunting.

7 When horses are free they live like wild animals but in vicinity of the hunter, so that he can observe them from time to time. This is a parallel to the way in which the hunter's prey lives somewhere in the forest.

8 In summer smoke from the fires provide protection against insects. In winter smoke is a sign for the horses that hunters are near and they are seeking contact with them. Most of the time horses also seek this contact in the hope of receiving something to eat (for example sweets and oats).

1

2

3

4

5

6

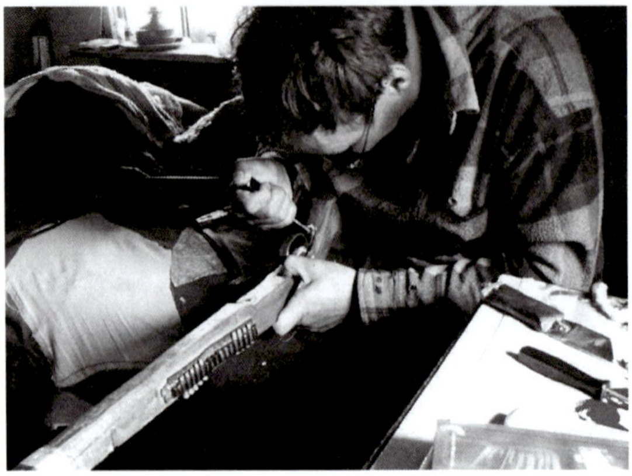

7

8. Guns in the Hunting Cycle

Guns are always present during all phases of hunting, but the hunter treats them differently during these phases. During the stage of anxiety, when the hunter is in the forest, the gun hangs on the hunter's back or from his horse, always within easy reach to shoot if prey should appear. During the excitement phase the gun is in his hands and is an extension of the hunter's body (for example, the telescopic sight provides an enhancement of the hunter's eyesight). The joyful phase is devoted to retrieving the prey and the gun is usually left standing nearby but also not in the centre of the camp that is organized at the location of a hunt. During the phase of calmness the gun is usually hanging outside on the cabin wall. From time to time the hunter cleans and repairs it. The position of the gun and its relation to the body of hunter most clearly marks the changes of mood. Anxiety is the experience of the gun hanging on the body. The excited hunter looks at the world through the gun's viewfinder guessing whether the shot is accurate. Joyfulness is when the gun is on the periphery of the hunter's perception. The state of calmness means the hunter has a lot of time to scrutinize the gun, clean and take care of it. Sometimes after cleaning, the hunter shoots at targets and adjusts the gun's accuracy. These episodes are predecessors of a new hunting cycle that bridge life after the hunt with preparations for new hunting.

1 Travelling on horseback the hunter can take two guns, one with a telescopic sight for hunting for meat and a light one for sable. In the event the hunter goes hunting on foot, he has to choose only one gun and so exclude the possibility of both types of prey. In such cases hunters frequently go in pairs and carry both guns. In this respect the horse is like the other man that carries the other gun.

2 Walking with a gun on your back indicates searching for an animal, when you need to be attentive to the environment and to react toward sounds and sights from all directions. Sometimes hunters carry guns hanging in front of them, and this means that they are tired, are not attentive to the surroundings and are not intending to shoot, because from this position it is more difficult to quickly take the gun in hand in the position for shooting.

3 The posture in which the hunter is aiming is unique to each individual. This depends on the environment, the weight of the gun and personal preferences. Women hunter find it easier to sit down.

4 The act of shooting takes place in a moment when all participants are looking at one point. This attention is materialized in the trajectory of the bullet.

5 After successfully shooting, the hunter takes a rest. He prepares hot tea and gives some refreshments to the dogs. The gun is left nearby at a point which can be seen as a kind of border between the imaginary territory of this improvised camp and the forest. It is left within the reach of the hunter in case of need, but it has lost its priority in his field of activities.

6 Cleaning a gun is such an emotionally appealing action, that although nothing spectacular happens during the procedure, all the bystanders watch how the hunter does it.

7 During hunting the gun goes through phases of attachment and detachment. The hunter investigates his gun as an interesting but strange object during the phase of calmness. He studies it and reassembles it.

1

3

2

4

5

6

7

9. Meat in the Hunting Cycle

Meat is the essence of life and is one of the main sources of pleasure and positive mood for the Evenki. The hunting cycle starts when meat runs out, and this lack is associated with a growing feeling of uncertainty and anxiety. The emotional tension that surrounds hunting for meat is substantially higher than for sable or squirrel hunting. Excitement is the phase when the hunter deals with an animal and not the meat; the transformation of an animal into meat happens in a second, when the animal is shot and dies. In the phase, when the animal is not a live creature any more but is also not yet butchered and rendered into pieces of meat, the hunter looks at the carcass with joy and admiration for some time. Usually dogs try to attack the carcass and the hunter has to tie the dogs at some distance from the place where the butchering takes place. After this episode, the animal is not an interactive partner, neither is it an object to be looked at and admired, but it has to be processed, transported and stored. The phase of calmness starts with all these tasks, which can be difficult (for example, skinning and butchering the carcass in the forest in winter when it is – 40 o C and has to be done with bare hands can be very unpleasant, besides, everything has to be done quickly before the meat is be frozen; loading heavy portions of meat onto the horse is very hard, to say nothing about having to carry it on one's back), but nevertheless they bring joy and satisfaction. Throughout this phase the amount of meat is decreasing, it is butchered and cut into smaller and smaller pieces. Hunters and other people that live in the taiga visit each other and if they come after a successful hunt , they frequently receive pieces of meat. Meat is also sent to relatives in the village and consumed at the campsite. When meat starts to run short, so the calmness starts to recede. Meat provides not only food, it is also a source of great entertainment partly because there are so many variations on how it can be cooked (eaten fresh, like liver, fried, grilled, boiled, cooked in pieces or minced, etc.). Cooking meat is one of the main entertainments during the phase of calmness, which is dominated by the boredom of tedious routine household tasks.

1 When meat runs out people go hunting, usually this happens when they have almost no food left. But reindeer herders are frequently supplied with canned meat which they take into the forest, when they go searching for reindeer.

2 The brown reindeer in the centre of this picture is a wild male that approached the herd of domestic reindeer during rut. Wild reindeer are seen as having more stamina in comparison to domestic animals. This is a perfect target for hunting because such animals come very close. Reindeer herders have to kill them not only for their meat, but also because they can lead female reindeer away from the herd.

3 Skinning is the procedure during which the animal is transformed into meat. This stage of processing brings joy partly because the amount of meat obtained becomes evident.

4 The same enjoyment is experienced after butchering, when before packing pieces of meat in sacks or storing it on a temporary platform in the forest, hunters leave it for a while on the ground to enjoy this sight. That is the moment to have a rest and smoke a cigarette.

5 In winter meat is usually stored in wooden boxes and people pack it into sacks only to transport it , for example, to the village to share with relatives. Quite large portions of meat are given away, if hunter can transport them into the village.

6 Cooking meat is a collective task, which involves everybody in the camp. Like cleaning guns, cooking meat is a pleasant task connected to the phases of excitement and joy during the long period of calmness.

7 Wild meat is never thrown away. People would prefer to eat spoiled meat rather than open cans of pre-cooked meat. Shashlik (chukin in Evenki) is a method of cooking fresh meat but also it is also a good way to prepare half spoiled meat, because fire and smoke conceal the smell.

1

2

3

4

5

6

7

10. Fur in the Hunting Cycle

The sable hunting cycle is less definite in comparison to hunting for meat, because in the latter case hunters go into the forest, when they do not have meat, and they stop hunting, when they have killed the prey. Hunters go hunting for sable, when they have time and the weather is appropriate. They do not stop hunting after bagging one sable; on the contrary, they work more intensively when their luck is good and they can take several sables. To stop hunting they have to feel that they've got all the sables they possibly could at this time. Sable hunting is much more about interaction between species, rather than about accuracy and skills, which are crucial in meat hunting. Sable hides in burrows, between stones and inside empty trees. To get the sable out of his hide, hunters and dogs need to work in cooperation. Sometimes they spend days trying to get the animal out. During all this time they can hear the sable snarling and the sable can hear peoples' voices and dogs' barking. The phase of excitement is filled with an intensive interaction between hunter, sable and dogs. This interaction is so impressive that the sable stays as an interactive partner even after being killed. The hunter plays with the carcass, teasing dogs and cats with it. For dogs, sable skin never loses its meaning as a hunting target. Hunters rarely wear fur caps and fur coats, partly because the dogs mistake them as the targets of hunting and refuse to go further in search of real animals. Hunting for sable is possible only during winter, which nevertheless is a long period between October and March.

1 After a sable is found and chased by the dogs, usually it hides under rocks in a burrow that has lots of exits. The hunter makes a fire in front of one of them and, using his clothes, fans the flames in such a way, that smoke from the fire infiltrates into the burrow. Places where the sable can escape suffocation are marked by the streams of smoke coming out. The dogs know that at this moment they have to be very attentive in order to catch the sable. Usually the sable manages to run out and climb up a tree. After this he is easily shot by hunter.

2 The cuts on this tree mark attempts to get at the sable that hid inside its trunk. As long as the hunters cut new holes the animal crawled further inside. Finally they had to cut the whole tree and caught the animal by hand. They did not even have to spend a bullet to kill it.

3 Traps are also a form of hunting for sable, but the Evenki do not like to come constantly back to the same place to check traps, and only set them near their camps.

4 After the sable is killed the hunter examines it very attentively. He looks at the quality and the colour of fur and also at the wounds to estimate the value of the pelt.

5 Playing with a cat and a sable's carcass is a source of great fun for this Evenki, because the cat catches the scent of a wild predator and gets scared, but is also curious. In this play hunting continues and the sable acts as an interactive partner in it, although now it is not prey but a kind of a hunter of the cat.

6 For several weeks skins are left hanging in the house to dry. Houses are small and these drying skins are always in sight; a proof and reminder of the successful hunt.

7 Reindeer is a unique prey because it provides not only meat, but also fur. Most popular are the skins from reindeer legs (kamus), because they are used to sew high fur boots.

1

2

3

4

5

6

7

1. Gathering various resources

When people are in the forest they frequently gather various things, from firewood to berries. This is one of the most routine and familiar activities, and is most egalitarian in its form, because everyone can collect and bring things home. The scheme for gathering is open to change: it is flexible enough to incorporate new objects and aims for gathering. Gathering does not need a concrete plan for the processing of gathered things: the latter can be left as a chaotic mass and stored. In this respect gathering provides an important buffer zone in the routine that creates a horizon for the activity of gathering, but does not lead to the immediate integration of this activity with further stages and plans. Gathering is relatively autonomous from other activities, in the sense that it does not inevitably cause other actions. You can store the gathered things or postpone the decision about what to do with them. This is why new things can be easily included in the list of things to gather. And this is also why gathering frequently is experienced as entertainment. Gathering itself does not contain a commitment to further action and this is why it suits the egalitarian ethos so well. Gathering is also a form of flexible practical categorization, in which actions are embodied thoughts about the distinction between desired objects and other stuff. This distinction is accomplished through the practice of separation (of the object from the stems, roots, branches and whatever obstacles), collecting together several objects of the same kind, carrying them somewhere and storing them for some time. The scale of things is in correlation with the capacities available to realise these actions. People develop their capacities to collect various objects and choose the objects to collect in accordance with their capacities. There is no direct cause and effect relationship between the scale and the capacity. Through gathering people create a potential to do something with the collected things.

1 When the reindeer herder comes home with the herd, several hundred metres before the forest edge, he starts to collect dry branches. These branches will help him to easily light a fire in the stove, so that the firewood will burn quickly and he can warm up the kettle to have tea.

2 Berries, cowberries in this case, are gathered with a special manual combine tool, an instrument that looks like a scoop with a metal comb.

3 At the top of the hill the hunter collects branches of redcurrant bushes, to make an aromatic tea with.

4 In winter, when the river is frozen, people use ice as a source of drinking water. The ice is chopped. Then blocks of ice are collected, transported and stored in front of the houses. People carry the blocks home and melt them in special barrels.

5 Moss is collected to interlay between the logs in building. Moss provides insulation.

6 Every year reindeer herders help the local vet to collect samples of reindeer's blood for analysis to inform a report about the state of health of the reindeer herd.

7 Ideally, assembling a satellite dish should be an opposite practice to gathering – it should be conducted with a clear plan of what is supposed to be the result. But when reindeer herders assemble whatever new device they happen to buy, usually they do not have any particular idea of the end product. Such assemblages quite often end up only half way completed, with the semi-assembled thing stored to be thought about at a later time. These projects are also experienced as puzzling entertainments. And their detachment from concrete purposes makes them akin to gathering.

1

2

3

4

5

6

7

8

2. Berries

Berries provide the most typical case for gathering. People are not the only creatures that collect berries; bears and reindeers eat them, squirrels and chipmunks collect and store them for winter. Gathering is a practice that is not exclusively human. Because the collection of berries is so widely shared, the effects of this practice are not so visible for people themselves. Berries are supposed to be collected and eaten by someone (it does not matter whether it is by animal or bird) and as such it is normal. When people collect berries they do not intrude or change the relationships between things in the ecosystem of the forest. What they do is that they occupy one of the possible niches and endanger other competitors who are also reliant on the same resource. People can change the environment and disrupt the existing order not by gathering berries per se, but by the scale of this practice. In the environment of the reindeer herders even the use of such instruments as manual combine tools that help to collect berries, do not provide people with the possibility to exhaust these resources. Here it is not the scale of the gathering practice that changes the environment, but the scale of the berry harvest that changes and affects the practice of gathering. The fact that this sensitivity exists is a sign that the limit, after which berry gathering is unsustainable, is reached.

1 The Cowberry (or Lingo berry) is one of the most popular, due to its taste and medicinal qualities. It is very well preserved under snow in winter and can be collected even at the beginning of summer, although then the berries are not plentiful enough to collect them for cooking. The main season for gathering is in August and September.

2 The Black Crowberry is a berry that is not very tasty to eat uncooked, but the jam is very good. The conserves made from these berries lower the blood pressure.

3 These cowberries were collected and stored in the moss by a chipmunk.

4 In summer people collect Wild redcurrants to make jams. In winter the branches of this bush are collected to make aromatic tea.

5 Dogs eat Northern Bilberries as well. In winter these berries remain on the branches of the small bushes above the snow cover. They are frozen and preserve all their taste and flavour.

6 Normally people collect berries sitting.This means that the quantity of berries is sufficient to justify staying in one place for a while.

7 When people search for a place to collect berries, they sometimes collect some berries on the way. This is relatively difficult, but at the same time it shows that there are not sufficient berries to justify sitting down and then standing up again. The collector has to move on to find a better place.

8 Sometimes there are so many berries that people can lie down and continue gathering. This is an indication that the place is particularly plentiful.

1

2

3

4

5

6

3. Firewood

The other essential item for people who live in the forest to collect is firewood. Because people have started to cut trees, instead of collecting dry branches, this practice leaves visible traces, as new trees take longer to grow than new branches. The damaging effects caused by people collecting berries and branches is remediated in a year, whereas the effect of cutting trees needs several years to be erased. Places where people have cut trees can be visibly recognized. They differ from other places, where the forest remains untouched. But at the same time there are other causes for similar damage, such as fires and storms, and even in this respect people do not create a new niche in the ecological system of destruction. Here they share this niche not with bears and reindeers, but with fires, storms and other factors that lead to deforestation. Territories that have been cleared of trees slowly become grassy plots or bogs, and are inhabited by various organisms.

1 Even now, when people live in houses with stoves, and not in tents, and make fewer open air fires, dry twigs are widely used to light the stove. This process needs to generate sufficient intensity of heat so that the logs, that are always a little bit damp catch alight.

2 In winter people cut trees at the level slightly above the snow, so that in summer the sizes of the stumps show what the levels of snow have been in past years.

3 A petrol-powered saw provides the opportunity for an individual to cut trees alone and to do it very quickly. But it is heavy and requires petrol, so its use is always bound to certain means of transport and reliant upon resources such as petrol.

4 An all-terrain military vehicle can fell trees just by crashing into them, and it also provides the opportunity to transport trees of all sizes, shapes and weights. But consequently people need at least a petrol-powered saw to cut these trees down into logs. Otherwise they need to spend an enormous effort to saw them manually.

5 The territory around a camp is deforested, and the bigger this area is, the longer people have been using this camp. Like the rings across a section of a tree can tell the whole story of the tree's development, so the landscape around a camp carries the details of the history of the camp.

6 There are some points, when technology is not available, and people cannot use petrol-powered saws. At this stage people start again to collect brushwood and twigs, and to manually cut small dry trees and even use stumps that have been left after the previous felling of trees. These stumps are leftovers. They have been discarded in the forest to wither, without any intention as to their future use someday. In this respect the potential that gathering as a practice creates is never fully seen and appreciated at the moment of collection. But at some future point this potential will unfold in the reality of its availability.

1

2

3

4

5

6

7

8

4. Searching and gathering

When people are gathering something, their attention is constantly switching between two logical types: the things themselves and groups of the things. To start gathering, people have to select a group of things to gather, then they gather these things one by one, and then start over again, searching for a new group of things to gather. A group of things might be represented by a cluster of berry plants covered with masses of berries, but it also can be a visually solid entity, such as a tree trunk. To cut down the latter you have to cut all the timber fibres, the more such fibres constitute one trunk, the more difficult it is to cut it. When people collect berries from one plant, or cut one trunk, they do not search for other groups of things, but monitor the work that they are doing to separate objects from their original environments. These moments of intensive attention to the group of objects are framed by another activity, notably the search for the next group to work with. This constant zigzag between the thing and the class of things, when people see trees and choose one particular tree, provides grounds for common confusions, when actions in these two modes overlap, for example, when people start to search for the next tree well before finishing off the cutting of the previous one. These situations can be dangerous, if people are dealing with tools such as saws, or ineffective, as when people look to collect berries in another place, where the distribution of berries is just as sparse and any investment of time in further searching, will just reduce the time spent on gathering. The main strategy to avoid such confusions is constant switching from one mode of attention to the other and back. This zigzag method of interchange in practice is so fundamental, that people continue on applying it in situations, where one of the modes of attention is not needed. For example, in the village, during chopping, people used to look around as if searching for something during the short pauses between chopping logs that have been already collected in one place. Such alternations in attention, from the particular object to the environment and back, also are seen as a rhythm for work, that helps to rest and economise strength.

1 Before starting to collect berries, a person needs to find a place where there are enough berries. For this, even the first place that seems to be good enough has to be compared with the surroundings.

2 When the person has collected enough berries and is packing things to go home, he takes one last look at the surroundings. This is done almost unconsciously, but provides an opportunity to remember the place and the density of berries, so as to be able to find a good place to collect berries the next time. This last look is taken in advance of the next gathering session.

3-4 The switching from collecting to searching happens all the time. People search not only for new places, but at the place where they are already searching, for new plants, and for new clusters of berries. So that there are lower and lower levels of abstraction, between which the person's attention shifts.

5-6 During sawing people have to mind not only issues relating to their own safety, but also risks for other people involved in the situation. The tree falls in a particular direction that can be determined by the way one is sawing. After the tree falls down, the person looks around to find a new tree and decide in which direction it should fall.

7-8 Chopping interchanged by looking around is a common case demonstrating the practice of constantly switching between doing and watching.

1

2

3

4

5

6

7

8

5. Instruments

The instruments that are used to separate the collected objects from their environments can be specialized or universal. Berries, for example, provide a very special configuration, so that there are no other parallels in the everyday life of people, and to collect berries people use a specially designed instrument. A combine tool can be relatively easily made at home through the transformation of other instruments, such as scoops. What people do with this instrument looks like brushing, during which berries are detached from their stems and collected in the scoop. This very specific design to some extent repeats the constitution of a human hand with some simplifications and changes that transform the practice and its orientation to the logical types. With a hand people tear off berries one by one, with a combine they scoop and filter, a cluster of berries at a time. This shift in the logical typing makes the procedure more efficient. Other instruments used in gathering are more universal, because on the one hand they compensate for a more general inability of a human body, and on the other hand they help to deal with tasks of a more general kind, such as the dividing of something into two parts such as a saw, or the breaking of something into pieces, such as an axe. The fact that such universal instruments can be useful in gathering shows that gathering as an intellectual task is based on elementary operations, such as the splitting of something into two parts and the carrying away one of the parts, or the breaking of a whole into a group of fragments, that can be collected and reassembled, not as previously complementary parts of something, but as members of a class. In this respect, gathering, no matter whether of berries or wood, is an act of reconstitution of the relationship between elements and the class of elements. Before gathering, berries are parts of the plant, they are representatives of the plant in its reproductive strategies, they contain seeds that can one day become plants with their own berries. After gathering, berries are individual autonomous things that due to their similarity in form, shape, colour and taste are identified as members of one class of berries. Their relation to the rest of the plant is severed, and a new relation with other berries is constructed. These new objects are located in the same place and probably most of them will share the same trajectory in the human consumption process.

1 A combine tool to collect berries looks like a scoop with brushing teeth, with additional holes in the middle to allow the leaves accidently detached with the berries to be sorted out.

2 People hold the combine tool with the thumb and index finger. Otherwise with these fingers people would pinch berries from the plant. The combine tool is not just an extension of the human arm, it is also a transformation of the whole body scheme of the practice and the logic of this action as well.

3 Sawing divides the tree approximately in the middle between its trunk and branches and its underground roots. This divide creates an opposition, in symbolical terms between top and bottom, in practical terms between the parts that humans can take and those that cannot be extracted from the ground.

4 Frozen meat is sawn to divide it into two parts. One part will be eaten; the other part will be stored. This is the creation of an opposition between consumed and stored, or between existing and not existing.

5 The petrol-powered saw makes it easier and faster to create new divisions and reorganize the relationships between elements that have been severed.

6 The axe is used to cut off the branches from the previously sawn trunk, so that the tree is transformed into a log and a heap of branches that do not have relations between each other anymore. Most often branches are just left in the forest lying on the ground with other branches that have been torn from the trees by winds.

7 An axe is used to chop bones to extract the bone marrow: splitting and separating the edible and the inedible.

8 Water in the barrel is frozen into ice. To use this water people have to chop the ice with an axe, then collect and melt down the chopped pieces.

1

2

3

4

5

6

7

8

6. Clearing and sorting things

Clearing and sorting out the things that have been collected is a meta-practice, because it is based on switching between different logical types of things to be collected from the environment (the wide set of things) to searching out unwanted things in the new set of collected things. During such sorting the collected berries become the context from which to extract the leaves and berries of bad quality. During clearing and sorting things people again gather. Gathering things and clearing them of junk are inversions of each other. In the former case people collect things they want from the environment they leave as unwanted. And in the latter case they collect elements they do not want to be present in the set of things they want. The shorter the path between gathering and consumption, the fewer are these inversions. For example, when people collect berries to eat, they compress gathering and clearing into one operation and collect them one by one, excluding leaves and rotten berries at the stage of gathering. When they have to collect more and faster, to store and consume later, they use a combine tool. Berries collected in this way are inevitably mixed with some leaves and have to be filtered and sorted out at later stages. Operations of logical typing need time to prevent confusions and paradoxes, and that is why all actions that are based on switches between logical types of things also inevitably need to take a certain amount of time. For example, people need dry firewood. There are two options here, either to cut trees without selection (but store the logs to dry - this can take a year), or to select dry trees only to cut from the beginning. You economize time on drying, because this process has already happened naturally before, but you have to spend time searching for such trees and then carrying the logs from different places. Time investment is unavoidable, although it can be optimized and reduced, but there is always a risk that either the cut trees will need more time to dry than planned, or that the dry trees you have chosen to cut will turn out to be not dry enough. Various techniques of gathering and potential possibilities of how to collect things show that every concrete instance of gathering is a two-fold process: it already contains a compression of gathering and clearing, but is also open to future elaboration, with new inversions. The gathered stuff can be cleared and recollected again and again.

1 To eat berries people collect them without leaves. But even the unseen process of digestion can be interpreted as a process of clearing and sorting out, with ongoing gathering.

2 When people scoop with the combine tool to collect berries they can sort the leaves out by blowing them away. Not only shapes and colour, but the weight and various other differences between things are used to identify, clear and filter the gathered things.

3-4 The collected berries undergo several relocations: they are put from the combined tool into a sack, then into a bucket, then are set out in the sun to dry, then are stored in a box in a cool place. Every such relocation is used as an opportunity to filter out the leaves and bad berries.

5 The cut tree is sawn into several parts, and branches are cut off with an axe. Through these clearing operations the tree is transformed into logs.

6 These parts of the log are initially set out in the forest to dry. They also are left in a position where they can be seen from a distance, so that they can be found once again later and taken home.

7 Some of the dry trees selected to be cut have already shed branches by themselves. These branches should not be cleared away as they can be used as firewood straight away. But people need some form of transport to collect them from the various locations where such trees were discovered.

8 The stump forms that piece of the tree that is left in the forest as the unwanted part. In time this piece of tree dries naturally and can be used as firewood too. When people do not have a means of transport to carry the logs home, they cut the stumps of the trees that are situated near the camp.

1

2

3

4

5

6

7

8

7. Laying out things and drying them

Drying is also a form of clearing and sorting things. During this procedure, the unnecessary water is evaporated from the collected objects. Drying takes time, which marks the division of a wet object into its dry part and water. To dry things they are usually laid out and are left exposed to contact with the air and sometimes to the sun's rays. Because the process of drying requires time and space, people need to introduce order into the organization of dried things, to reduce the space needed and to guarantee a certain level of air circulation. Visually things that are left to dry present a mixture of order and disorder. On the one hand things are organized according to some symmetrical patterns, on the other these patterns provide an opportunity to compare the collected things and to see their unique differences. All berries laid out together are of more or less the same colour, but a closer inspection shows that there is always some subtle difference in tint. This cannot be seen without putting the berries together. In the forest berries all look red, for example, because people compare them not with other red things, but with the green and grey moss, with the yellow, needle-like leaves of larch, and with the brown rocks. The process of drying can be initiated and supported through the organization of things and the layout, but it cannot be easily stopped or controlled. Some things continue drying all the time and should be consumed before they become too dry. Or some things cannot be dried at all, and the process of drying is simply a way of slowing down rotting. In this case such things also have to be consumed within a certain time. To control the processes of drying or rotting, people have to reorganize the things left out to dry from time to time, changing the order, moving portions of things into other places and correcting changes in the environment.

1 Dry twigs are things that have been cut from the internal circulation processes of a tree due to some non-human cause. These twigs have been left to dry by themselves. People collect them to use immediately to light their stoves. There is no need to allocate additional time and space to process such materials.

2 Before making jam, berries are set out to dry. This procedure not only helps to prolong the period of rotting for the berries, but also to make clearing simpler. The dried leaves can be easily identified and detached; they do not stick to the berries any more.

3 Herbs are hung up in the attic to dry. These drapings are funny toys for a kitten to play with.

4 People put moss between logs to insulate buildings. Both logs and moss continue dry and to rot. In this respect all buildings in the forest are displays of the materials from which they are built, that are left to dry and rot away.

5 The pieces of ice set out in front of the house are of course not left there to dry. This is a way to store the stocks of drinking water in winter. Rapid changes of temperature rather than stable cold lead to the fusion of parts into a frozen mass.

6 During hunting various things that are left out to dry are frequently collected together in one place. Freshly cut wood to heat the hunting cabin; a saddle and the fresh skins of squirrels and a sable function as layers for each other. On top are the most fragile and precious things. Every layer of drying things also plays the role of insulating pad for the layer above.

7 People cut logs into shapes that are easy to stack in a pile. The shape of things is suitable for three main operations: to store wood in compact piles in the yard, to carry the logs also in compact piles on a hand cart, and to make a smaller pile of logs inside the stove in order to burn them.

8 Various reorganizations are routine tasks that can be easily carried out by children. To reorganize things so that elements change positions but the overall order stays the same is a playful task.

1

2

3

4

5

6

7

8

8. Transport and containers

Gathering can be defined as a task of concentrating things that are scattered, and then moving this concentration to the place you need it to be. This twofold aim of gathering explains why often the container in which things are collected and the means of transport are adjusted to each other. In the forest the main means of transport is usually a human being, who carries the container (a bucket for example), drags sledges, or carries bound heaps of things on his or her back. When people carry containers with things that they have gathered, they form a kind of a moving whole. Usually during gathering the container is put aside to collect scattered things. Sometimes, like in the case of collecting mushrooms, people collect along the way. When they put the container down on the ground it becomes an object with a special status. Its main role is to secure the collected things, and there is a kind of gravitation that appears around it. People collect new items and put them into the container, more and more objects pass the same centripetal trajectory. The container, not being the main focus of attention for people who are involved in searching and gathering things, forms a centre for the situation of gathering. People do not go far away from the container, put other things that they do not need for gathering (such as guns or pots) near it, sit near the container during pauses and smoke breaks. Any means of transport, such as a tractor, also forms the same centre as a potential container. The container is not the focus of attention, but it is the vital centre of a field of actions. Without the container people do not have a place to search around and come back to. The paradox of the container is that it swallows things (like a black hole), but is not visible itself. People do not look at the container, when they search and collect things, but they need to know that there is such a central point; they themselves should be unfocused on it to be able to find things to put in it. In this sense, the container does not provide feedback, as long as it has the capacity to swallow more and more things. Only when it is full and its role as the focal point of centripetal forces is completed, does the container transform into a solid object that now has to be transported to the desired destination. From then on it is not its capacity to collect things within itself that makes it central, but its weight and inertia that make this object the focus for people's actions.

1 The term 'container' can be misleading, as sometimes it is just a rope that helps to hold collected logs together.

2 Sledges are typical examples of the mutual adjustment of container and means of transportation.

3-4 In the case of logs transported by tractor and by all-terrain vehicle it is the strong wire that holds the logs together and attaches them to the dragging vehicle.

5 Once the bucket is full it has to be covered, so as to insulate it along with its content from possible interference during the transportation.

6 There are two ways to carry the container on the back: either to attach the shoulder straps directly to it, or to put the container inside the backpack.

7 The plastic barrel with a cover is not even taken out of the backpack. People gather close to the place where they leave it.

8 During the lunch-break people stay near the container.

1

2

3

4

5

6

7

9. Buckets

A bucket is the most useful container in which to collect things and carry them home. The capacity to contain is always important and is on demand. On the way into the forest people carry the instruments with which they collect berries (a combine tool, a plastic sack to lay berries out for selection, etc.) in a bucket, on the way back they carry these things in their hands along with the bucket filled with berries. Regarding this we can say that the bucket is an object that can play multiple roles in the logical typing of gathering. It is a conundrum that appears both on the level of instruments, being one of them, and on the level of collecting instruments, being used as a container to carry instruments. The bucket is a meta-object that plays the role of a meaningful context for gathering. It frames the situation of gathering for so long as it is capable of storing more berries, and it frames the gathering as a distinct activity by being used as an instrument to transport the instruments for gathering to the locus of action (collecting berries) and then as a container of berries, as they are transported back home. The bucket is created and adjusted to the human body and its ability to carry things. Usually people need a couple of hours to fill the bucket with berries. Usually this is exactly the amount of time that they feel comfortable to spend gathering. If it took longer, they would probably feel tired. The bucket filled with berries weighs between 5 and 8 kilograms and this weight is commonly accepted as being easy to carry for some distance. The capacity of the bucket to contain from 5 to 8 kilograms of berries is a function of the time spent collecting and the strength to be able to carry. All these parameters relate to capacities of the human body. This explains why buckets are so widely used in households too, for collecting and carrying water, in milking and in cooking.

1 A combine tool and other instruments for collecting berries are kept inside the bucket. The future berry-container contains the instruments with which these berries will be collected. Gathering starts, when these instruments are taken out and the bucket becomes an empty container, open for collecting in.

2 On the way back all the instruments are carried in individuals' hands, and the bucket with its top covered by a sack for insulation contains only berries.

3 The bucket is stable. It can be left standing by itself on the ground. But uncovered it always runs the risk of being knocked over. Just as it is open to receive berries, it is also open to spilling the collected things out.

4 Sometimes people do not collect straight into the bucket, but onto the sack. They then sort the berries and take out the leaves.

5 Cleaned berries are poured into the bucket from the sack.

6 Buckets are good for collecting ingredients for baking bread and kneading dough.

7 A bucket is the best container in which to collect milk during milking.

1

2

3

4

5

6

7

10. Consumption

The ultimate goal of gathering is consumption. For immediate consumption people collect relatively moderate amounts of things. The longer the time span between gathering and consumption the bigger the quantities of things collected. Immediate consumption is experienced as pleasant and entertaining, but it is frequently not the focal activity but a kind of entertaining moment embedded in other mainstream activities. For example, whilst collecting berries people from time to time eat them. And although all berries are collected to be eaten some day, in the frame of gathering, immediate consumption is not part of the practice but marks a short break taken to have a rest. Consumption in other circumstances also frequently performs the function of entertainment, for example treating oneself to jam before departure or during a break in doing household chores. Various forms of gathering can overlap, and they are usually coordinated in such a way, that collecting for immediate consumption continues to be instrumental for the purposes of collecting for postponed consumption. For example, people can collect wood for the fire to cook lunch during a break in berry gathering. In immediate consumption people are less constrained and can select what they like to consume, for example, setting up the fire to cook lunch, they might collect dry branches that will burn fast and easy. But for later, people would collect trunks to set up the fire in the stove, they would chop these trunks into thin sticks. They would produce things from this chopping instead of collecting separate branches. Collection for postponed consumption presupposes the possibility to adjust the collected things for various types of use in the future, while the collection for immediate consumption is based on a straightforward ongoing selection of collected things for the immediate purpose.

1 Eating berries during berry collection is a moment when people rest. These are moments when the main goal of collecting (consumption) intrudes and disrupts the actual practice of collection, thus generating a paradox and overlap of two planes of action, aimed respectively at the short and long terms.

2 Hot tea, bread and jam made from berries are the main snacks for pauses in work, but they are also entertainments that divert people from boredom and routine.

3 A stop along the way to have a cigarette, a toilet break and to eat berries from the plants that grow on the side of the track.

4 During berry collection people also pause to cook lunch in the forest and to collect firewood.

5 Sticks are cut from the logs that were themselves chopped trunks. These thin wooden sticks help to start the fire in the stove. For immediate consumption in the forest people would not need these chains of work, instead they would just collect dry branches.

6 The principle of postponed consumption is also applied to the consumption procedure itself. People warm themselves by staying close to the fire in the forest. But at home people let the fire warm the stones and bricks of the stove and only then get warm by staying near the stove or inside the house.

7 Ribbons are smoked on the fire in the forest. The logs for the fire were chopped and burnt immediately. Rituals frequently consist of short term consumption sequences.

1

2

3

4

5

6

7

8

11. Ice and Jade

There is a striking parallel between how ice and jade are treated in this region. Ice is the main source of drinking water in winter. People break up the ice in the river, collect pieces, transport them home and set them out on wooden platforms. At home people have iron tanks where they leave pieces of ice and let them melt. Jade is a semi-precious stone that is extracted from the mountain by open-cast mining. The mountain is dynamited and the resultant pieces of jade are transported to the mining camp and stored on wooden platforms. Then the jade is transported in all-terrain vehicles to the places where it is sold to Chinese buyers. People gain enormous profits which, however, vanish into the air and disappear without trace, like the water from the ice. Jade extraction is a new occupation for the region, before the 1990s it was not even known that there was a deposit of white jade that is valued in the neighboring China. The fact that people organize the extraction of the jade as a copy of the ice collection could be both a coincidence and an intuitive recognition of the commonalities between water and jade, with the only difference being that these substances circulate on different scales of consumption. Water is ultimately consumed by people in their daily routines, and jade is consumed somewhere far away. Local people do not know how exactly it is consumed by itself. When jade is sold and transported to China people are left with money but no information about the life of the jade afterwards. This disappearance is comparable with the melting of ice, when firm, vigorously shaped pieces of solid ice melt and become water, without color or stable form.

1 Usually ice is smashed and broken up with axes.

2 Dynamite is put inside drilled holes in the mountain rock.

3 Pieces of ice are set out in front of the house on a wooden platform, from which it is easy to take pieces and carry them home to melt into water.

4 In the mining camp pieces of jade are stored on wooden platforms similar to those constructed for ice.

5 Ice is transported by tractors.

6 Jade is transported by all-terrain vehicles, as the routes are through the forest where there are no roads.

7 The pieces of ice are heavy and very cold, so it is quite uncomfortable to carry them.

8 Jade is very heavy. Some pieces can only be carried by several men.

1

2

3

4

5

6

7

8

12. Gathering and Packing Things

Collecting and gathering happen not only when people collect resources such as food or fuel. Every journey starts with collecting and gathering things to be taken. In the region of this study ,travelling is an integral part of people's lives and a substantial amount of time is spent on gathering and packing things in this regard. Such collecting differs from previously described forms of gathering as it is based on hesitation, the doubtful thoughts about what to take and what to leave. Gathering things before a trip is an action which attempts a balance between the open variety of possible future needs and the limited capacities of the means of transport. Hesitation is absent from the general process of collecting resources because people not only gather them but also always extract them from their previous context. The capacity to transport such things usually does not imply the risk of leaving substantial things behind, because such collections are always surpluses to basic belongings. When they travel, people frequently have to carry essential elements of their personal belongings that play important roles in their lifestyles. Any decision has its effect not only on future consumption processes, but also on future collection processes. People have to decide what instruments to take, and this decision defines what they will be able to collect in the future. We cans say that collecting things before going somewhere is a framing practice, the meta-level in relation to the practice of collecting and gathering resources. People collect instruments to go to collect resources. And they collect resources to be able to collect instruments and so forth. Things collected also go through these logical typing procedures. Berries are taken to the village to be given as a gift to the hosts that provide people with a place to stay in the village. During these stays people collect and maintain contacts with other people. They find bullets to go hunting or they buy a new bucket. Instruments that help people to collect things are exchanged for things that have been collected by them. These are the logical loops of gathering and collection that help to reiterate cycles of these activities.

1 People gather around individuals preparing to go away. They share their hesitation about what is worth taking and what should be left behind.

2 People look at the heaps of things that they plan to take and think how to pack them. These are decisions that take time to be made.

3 Animals participate in these decisions as they show their eagerness to carry things. Even their passive presence helps people to keep in mind that what they take will be carried by a living creature with its own capacities and risks.

4 All-terrain vehicles are less involved in such decisions due to their almost inexhaustible capacity to transport things. People usually do not have more things in total than the all-terrain vehicle can carry. Vehicles are instruments that help to collect and transport instruments that will be used to collect other things.

5-6 Animals carry things that people have loaded onto them. Animals have the capacity to carry things because they themselves do not need instruments to collect food, neither do they need the infrastructure for storage. In this region people do not collect and transport hay or moss for the horses and reindeer which they use to transport their own instruments and storages. Otherwise there would no place for the human belongings and animals would carry only their own collections.

7-8 People live in camps and go on their trips to gather resources with only those things that they need for their limited tasks. They leave all other various instruments behind at the camp.

1

2

3

4

5

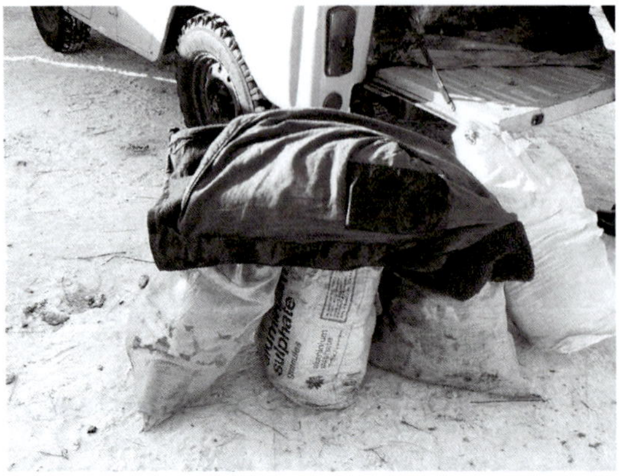

6

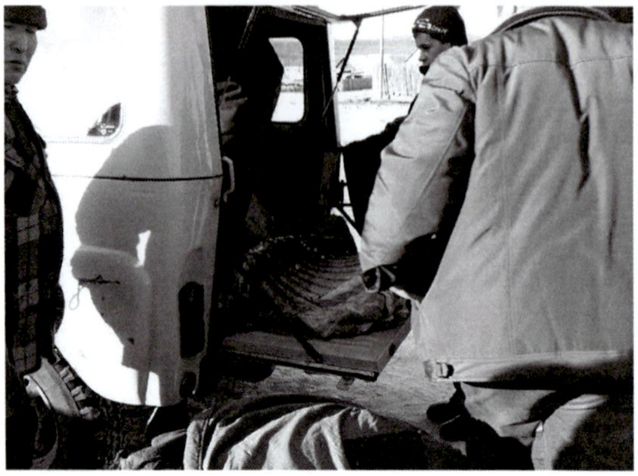

7

13. Containers of Disorder

Packing things consist of several stages that we can designate as stages of order and disorder. First of all, people collect things that they think they will need from their camp environment, then they lay them out to estimate the quantities and make decisions, what to take and what to leave. These stages replicate the same process as with collecting berries or wood and then laying out them to dry, clear and select. These actions aim to create new groups and categories of things, first the general group of stuff to be taken on the journey, and then the sub-groups of things put into different sacks and bags together. These operations in logical typing – switches from members of the classes (or groups) to classes of classes and back – designate the relationship between logical types and highlight the question of chaos (or disorder) versus order. When people deal with the environment from which they extract things, this environment shows itself as disordered. The moment when people collect things they need together, is the moment of order, i.e. a pattern or a sequence of repetitive actions. But as soon as people have collected these things together, they once again return to chaos, a group inside which there is no order, and people have to create this new order, by dividing the initial group into sub-groups according to their places in bags and sacks. The moment of switching from one logical type to another is the moment of order, and this is also the moment that divides two different disorders. Order is a black box by itself; we have the input of the first group of things with its chaotic and unorganized pattern of collocation, and we also have the output – another type of chaotic co-location of the things. Inside the black box we can try to recognize patterns and sequences that have supported the transduction process. But we will just realize that inside the black box of order there are more and more new black boxes that contain stages of order and disorder. Every process of packing can be subdivided into smaller and smaller sequences of interchange of collecting, displaying and recollecting (or selecting).

1 The chaos of things set out on display before packing into bags. People experience the openness of chaos to ordering through hesitation.

2 Things are regrouped and put into bags. Although from afar these bags look more ordered in comparison to the previous picture of the lay out, they still contain groups of things that can be seen as disordered, and can be unpacked and redistributed between bags.

3 The phase of display can contain internal regroupings, for example, when glass jars are grouped together separately from plastic bottles. These orders have no sense in relation to the repacking process, because glass objects cannot be put together due to the risk of smashing. So what looks like order can also be a case of disorder in respect to new criteria.

4 When things are packed into different sacks the new stage starts. This is when sacks (that contain things and are material groups of things) are displayed and people group various sacks together to find the perfect match between sacks, bags and horses that will carry all this.

5 Finally all things are packed, and the disorders that sacks contain are covered by bags. These are black boxes of order that once unpacked can be seen as containers of disorder.

6 Sometimes things are isolated in sacks inside these containers of disorder to avoid contact with other disorders. For example clothes are isolated from meat.

7 But these segregations can be rearranged so that pieces of meat are put inside the car as they are, without packing them into sacks. So the car itself becomes a kind of container of disorder.

1

2

3

4

5

6

7

8

14. Gathering and Atmosphere

People experience a wide range of emotions, from hesitation to joy, when they deal with the task of collecting things. The person who gathers something, for example, who collects things before departure, attracts the attention of others. People gather around the person who gathers. The operation of switching between logical types opens potential for the expansion of this shift into higher meta-levels of organization and communication. The person has to deal with a logical operation to select and collect different things into one group and create relationships between several of such groups, and this person collects other people around him to deal with this task more efficiently. The operation of collecting things ultimately collects people who collect things. This cascade patterning creates an atmosphere, which can be defined as a bundle or dense entanglement of elements that refer to different logical types. A special atmosphere of gathering is created when people try to make order out of chaos, because through these attempts they increase complexity and create cross-cutting relations between logical levels. By picking up things and assembling them together they create a new thing, which consists of collected things. And this new thing leads to new possibilities and potentials to relate to other things of its kind. The thing is a bundle of new possibilities: possibilities to share collected things, to store them, to transport them and to carry out other actions, which were not possible so long as things were not yet collected. People feel that there is a kind of special atmosphere that surrounds gathering, and what they feel is hesitation, joy or anxiety. These are emotions devoted to the experience of this openness of the situation to new possibilities. They mark the shift to a meta-level of communication and practice.

1 Men gather before starting to butcher the carcass of a calf and dress the meat. They drink beer and chat. The hard work for which they are preparing is anticipated with enthusiasm.

2 Later the men cut the meat into pieces, and order the internal organs, tissues and bones according to future storage plans, consumption and exchange. Parts of the carcass become separate things that then are reassembled and collected again into new categories and groups.

3 When a relative comes from a distant village, people welcome him with various delicacies. They collect this food from neighbors and friends and they themselves gather at the table. The atmosphere of joy is a result of this recollection, when people who are usually separated are brought together.

4 The sacred ritual of offering of food to the spirits consists of the collection of delicacies. People gather samples of all the foods they like and offer them to the spirits. The event is experienced as joyful.

5 Packing things into the car is a time not only to think collectively about how to pack things better, but it is also the last opportunity to spend time together. Packing gives people the possibility to say goodbye without saying anything, just by helping and assisting to collect things properly. Such gatherings can be not only joyful, opportunities to be together and make final jokes about each other, but also sad and full of anxiety.

6 What to take and what to leave, what things to pack together and what packs to load on which horses, all these are decisions that people make together. People who are going and people who are staying have an equal say in this process. This is due to the interchangeability, because there have been (and there will again be) other occasions when people needed to resolve the same problems, although others were travelling away and others were staying.

7-8 When people feel bored and want to entertain themselves, they make home brew with sugar and yeast. Sometimes they add berries to improve the aroma and taste. Alcohol provides a substitute for the actual atmosphere of reuniting. Light drunkenness is a state in which people feel as if they have gathered something. They also feel the joy and enthusiasm of being part of a collection, as if some force has gathered them with others into new categories or groups, and new potentialities for communication and collaboration have been opened to them.

1

2

3

4

5

6

15. Gathering Chaos

Gathering and collecting would not be possible without disorder and chaos. Things should be extracted from the chaotic environment to become bits of information about the new order in which they are assembled. And once things are recollected and reorganized, the previous order in which they were put should be abandoned and identified as chaos. Order and disorder are interchanging environments of the practice of collecting. We can see that the practice of collecting is something that takes place between two distinct states of disorder. When people start gathering, they operate in a chaotic environment of things (that is how you need to see it to be able to propose a new order for the selected things), and when they finish, what they have is a group of things they have collected, which can itself be seen as a chaotic environment for new operations of selection and gathering. These chaoses refer to different levels of logical types. And gathering (or collecting) is an operation that generates the relation between them. Such gathering is always open to paradoxes. People need again and again to collect things or recollect previously collected objects, because either the aims for which the storages were created change, or the collected things themselves change. All these changes are the spores of chaos that continuously recast the order that people implement.

1 As children grow up from time to time things that are too small for them should be packed into wardrobes, and things that they are now big enough for should be taken out. These reorganisations, when people unpack and pack things without travelling, do not happen often, but at least once a year.

2 Things previously collected also do not remain unchanging for long. People take potatoes out of the wooden box, where they keep them, and cut off the shoots. The rotten potatoes are sorted out.

3 Numerous sacks and bags hang on the outside wall of the hut. Inside these bags people store important things that they have previously collected: medicines, food stuffs, various instruments and materials. From time to time people reorganize these storages to maintain them in order. If left unattended, these storages will revert to disorder.

4 Repairing is also a case of recollection. People check for problems, search for break downs and disassemble the machinery they want to repair. First they collect information about its structure and all the details of its functions. After the problem is identified (hopefully), they reassemble the mechanism. Often they introduce their own hand-made substitutions for the missing pieces, because it is almost impossible to find spare parts. As a result the mechanism they reassemble is different from the one they were trying to fix. There is no guarantee that the fixed mechanism will work properly. And there is not any device or vehicle that can be fully relied on.

5 The reindeer herd is also changing all the time. Each time herders collect their reindeer and drive them home, the herd is different. Some reindeer stay in the forest, others that have been absent for a long time reunite with the herd and return home.

6 The best parties happen when somebody arrives at the camp. The next day some people who have been staying at the camp depart, using the transport that brought last night's arrivals. The party is a moment of gathering that unites those who are about to leave with those who have just arrived.. And it is also a moment of recombination, when the group of residents of the camp changes.

1

2

3

4

5

6

7

8

1. Reindeer and People

Those Evenki who are involved in reindeer herding are constant observers of various events in reindeer life. Any contact with reindeer is experienced as a pleasure; people wait for the herd to come home and are happy to see the animals. These positive emotions are expressions of the relationships that obtain between reindeer and Evenki people. On the one hand animals and people do not intrude into each other's lives. People do not exploit reindeer the way they might use domestic cattle, and reindeer themselves impose few obligations on people – they do not need to be feed. People can leave the animals to go free most of the time, without any guidance. On the other hand, people and animals gain many benefits from living together: people have the opportunity to kill wild reindeer attracted by the herd, and reindeer can live in peace protected from wolves. The relationship between Evenki and reindeer can be called a symbiosis, in which neither people nor reindeer play dominant role. As a result it is easy to see common features in their lives, and Evenki happily recognise their own character traits in reindeer.

1 Reindeer don't come home at a fixed time; there is no schedule. The frequency with which reindeer come to the camp also changes with the seasons. In summer, when only the smoke from people's fires can protect from insects, reindeer appear at camp more often. Each appearance of the herd from the forest is appreciated and welcomed. People watch happily how animals are coming home.

2 Letting reindeer go free after enclosing them for a while is an even more pleasurable event. Life at camp is punctuated by these two types of emotionally appealing events in which reindeer come and go.

3 Occasions when usually peaceful reindeer show aggressive behavior are also greeted with excitement. People compare reindeer fighting in a fair competition among themselves.

4 Scenes of mothering constitute the other important affective stimulus, when people see their own love of their babies reflected in the reindeer. They feel that they understand the animals and share common features with them.

5 It is very difficult to establish a boundary between domestic and wild features of reindeer. An animal may sometimes be so tame it may try to enter a house.

6 Sometimes wild reindeer come to the camp attracted by the scent of females from the herd. This is the moment when they can easily be killed. And this is also an opportunity to compare wild and domestic reindeer, to see that the wild reindeer are fitter, and to notice whether they carry any features of domestic relatives that escaped from the herd some years ago.

7 Although nowadays reindeer are rarely used for transportation, they are still the most reliable form of transport, requiring no expensive fuel, not breaking down in the middle of nowhere, and able to traverse all terrains, from mountains to swamps.

8 Milking reindeer is also becoming a rare practice. People prefer not to disturb the animals if they have other sources of milk. They even prefer to use dry powdered "milk" made from soya beans, rather than catch and milk animals. But if even this substitute is unavailable, then milking is practiced.

1

2

3

4

5

6

2. Reindeer without people

During most of the daylight hours, which reindeer spend free in taiga, they are constantly on the move and eating either grass, moss or mushrooms. Their movements help to avoid putting too much pressure on the environments, so that the behaviour of reindeer minimises the risk of change and destruction of their grazing lands. Although they move along several routes around the valley, reindeer choose different places to forage each day. This enables them to stay in a shared environment but not to be bound to any particular point, so that predators (and people) cannot easily find them. The only fixed place is a human camp, where the reindeer obtain protection from wolves. In the forest or even on the plain reindeers become part of the environment, not opposed to it, but facilitating to the environment constitution. Everything that reindeer do, when people are not involved, is part of the creation of an environment in which they live. Their constant eating and moving balances the relationship between them and their world.

1 Although it is a given among people that winter is the harshest season, for reindeer the coldness of winter is probably not much more difficult than summer with its annoying insects. Winter is the time when reindeer especially use their sense of smell to uncover moss and berries under snow. The hardest time is at winter's end, when a thin crust of ice over the snow makes digging painful and difficult.

2–3 In this respect autumn is the most affluent time, with berries, mushrooms and moss all over the place. Exactly at this moment reindeer start rutting. Males sometimes even stop eating for a month and spend this time fighting with each other and courting. This lasts not more than a month and then animals turn back to their routine search for food.

4 Summer may be hot or rainy, but it is always a time of constant irritation from insects. Running through bushes and brushing against their protruding branches provides little help. Problems and solutions are integral to the reindeer environment. If insects and heat are features of the local ecosystem, so are fresh air and breezes at high altitudes in the mountains which provide relief from both problems.

5 Drinking is a very individual practice for reindeer. Reindeer graze together, but never drink simultaneously from the same pool of water. Probably this prevents epidemics, but at the same time this is an attitude that shows that their relationship with water is of a special kind. Drinking is a moment, when the animal is totally involved and cannot control what's happening around it. For this reason it is safer if only one animal at a time is fixed on drinking while others keep watch.

6 Crossing a river or a stream is a stressful moment, mainly because of the risk of slipping. Just like when it drinks, it is also a period when the reindeer is highly concentrated on its own movements and cannot remain aware of what is around it. All difficult crossing points and traverses carry potential risks, not only of because of accidents, but also because of the attention animals have to pay to the task at hand.

7-8 The pace of reindeer movement through the forest correlates with their mood, the weather condition and quality of food they find. These movements are so firmly embedded in the local environment that by themselves reindeer manage to hide in the forest, i.e. to be part of the environment and not stand out to the observer as a figure against the background.

1

2

3

4

5

6

7

8

3. Herd

The reindeer herd is not just a group of individual animals but a communicative system, in which goals are formed, uses the sense organs of all animals to communicate and receive signals from outside the herd. Reindeer eat and move, all the while communicating with each other, so that the behavior of an individual animal is impossible to understand without looking at other animals. Visually this can most easily be seen from a distance, especially on open planes, when the herd looks like one continuously moving body with scores of legs and antlers. From close up, the herd looks more like a flow of animals that streams across plains and through the forest. The direction that this flow takes depends on a circuit relationship between changes in the environment (surface, smell, sound, sight) and the intention of the herd to find food and avoid risks.

1 The herd is not structured hierarchically, so there is no leading animal that sets a direction for others to follow. But when several reindeer simultaneously find an attractive patch of grass or moss, their involvement shows others which way to go. As a result animals do not move in the same direction, but they eat in the same direction. They stay so close to each other that they can feel each other kinaesthetically.

2 Movements of the herd depend on the shapes and forms of the environment, so that the external environment, which poses obstacles for animals moving together and keeping time, always disrupts the unity of a herd. The herd has to adapt to the landscape and adjust itself in such a way, that parts of the environment that prevent its unity can be temporarily integrated into the form of the herd. Like the slope of the hill that makes the body of the herd into a salient.

3 The herd is egalitarian. This means that any member of the herd can give an impulse to others to move in a particular direction. From the moving vanguard, reindeer form a line perpendicular to the direction of movement. This line is continuously superseded by another line, formed by other reindeer, which set another perpendicular direction for the herd's trajectory.

4 If food is an attractive aim, then other creatures (if they are big enough to pose a threat) can also have influence on the herd's behavior. People use this sensitivity, and by chasing reindeer redirect the movements of the herd towards the camp.

5 When going through bushes animals are in proximity to each other but can mostly only smell and hear other reindeer. To avoid the risk of losing someone, reindeer cross bushes very fast and never stay there for long, even if they find the leaves rather tasty. Bushes are a boundary to cross and not a place to graze. In this situation, members of the herd become especially attentive to each other and that makes the herd more coherent.

6 Rivers form a similar kind of barrier (or boundary) for the herd, if not because of limited visibility, then for the risk of slipping and breaking a leg. The reindeer's strategy in this situation is contradictory, because they try to cross the river as fast as possible, just as they run through the bushes, but this hurry makes the crossing even more risky.

7 When walking through the forest, where moss doesn't grow as densely as grass on the plain, reindeer have to keep a distance between each other, but at the same time not to lose the herd's coherence.

8 From a distance it is possible to see that although the herd is not so compact in the forest, it still demonstrates the same form as in the open valleys. This impression is much strengthened when you see its homogeneous movements.

1

2

3

4

5

6

4. Following one reindeer

Communication inside the reindeer herd happens in such a way that if any one reindeer shows a consistent inclination to go in a particular direction this is accepted as a pattern that others should follow. The reason for this direction is not included into the message delivered to other animals, but only the direction and the force with which the particular animal is eager to go there. This is used by people to direct the movement of the herd by catching and carrying one animal on a leash or attracting an animal by showing it food. There is no difference which animal the person chooses, the herd will follow any of its members that at some point starts moving in a particular direction set by the reindeer herder. But usually people find their own favourites to catch from the herd (whether because it is easier to catch or a person has a particular relationship to one animal) and thus they construct a kind of role of a mediating reindeer between the herd and the person. It seems that the herd never becomes aware of the hierarchy that people impose on it and just follow the animal without attributing it any particular status or role. The egalitarian pattern of communication between reindeer does not contain distinction between different animals that provide signals and even between different meanings of signals (running for food or running from danger), but only the reaction to the signal and an attempt to accommodate it and adjust the trajectory of the herd. The willingness of an animal to go in a particular direction is always balanced by its willingness to follow others, if in the case of one particular reindeer this balance is disturbed, than for the herd this means that the animal probably has good reasons and the whole herd should consider this as a sign and follow. This factor also explains why the reindeer continue to follow the same animals that are habitually used by people and not disregard their signals as unauthentic. The egalitarianism of reindeer communication is evidenced in the trust that herd has toward every member.

1 Leading the whole herd on one leash is probably the most impressive performance of the way people subordinate the herd to themselves.

2 Not only walking away but also staying in one place can be a signal. Reindeer herders sometimes bind the reindeer by which they led the herd at the campsite to ensure that the herd stays at the camp for some time. They never do it for too long, as animals need to be let free to find food.

3 Even the relocation of the bound reindeer effects the movements of other animals. Although they walk around freely the bound reindeer becomes a kind of centre of gravity for the herd, particularly because the continuity of his behaviour becomes a source of information for others.

4 When reindeer herders have mixed fodder than they do not even need a rope. They can just show a sack of this fodder to make the herd follow it.

5 Usually the herder attracts one or two animals, and other animals follow them.

6 To support this pattern the reindeer herder leads the herd into the fence where he gives the fodder to animals. In this case he does not bind one animal, but enclose the whole herd. In this case the herd is reduced to a group of independent individuals because the enclosed territory is too small to orchestrate manoeuvres and there is no need to be constantly attentive to the directions of others.

1

2

3

4

5

6

5. The camp landscape

The landscape of the camp is fragmented. There are a lot of things just lying on the ground, left there because they were broken or because the particular plans connected with them did not lead to action. The contexts and histories of these things are lost in everyday routine but at the same time they do not merge into one layer, they are not yet seen as undistinguishable. And this fragmentation of the landscape at the camp leads to a change in the organization of the herd. When the herd comes to the camp it breaks up. Reindeer wander around as individuals, themselves fragments of the herd. At the camp reindeer receive salt and forage, and hide from insects in the smoke made by people. Usually, if the reindeer are free, they do not stay at the camp for long. The camp provides a source of essential acids which are very difficult to find outside in such concentrations. The more concentrated the forage the less time reindeer need to consume it. Following this, we can say that time speeds up for reindeer at the camp. There is no normal forage (like grass or moss) to restore the normal temporal rhythm, and when people keep reindeer inside the fence for hours the animals experience it as sense of void (characterised by an absence of tasks, dangers and space). The comfort that a camp environment provides is principally built on disintegration and communication breakdown. Animals do not have the texture of events to communicate about with each other. This can be compared with the situation of weightlessness or zero gravity, in which objects loose contact with each other, abandoning their previous organisation and become individuals with their own trajectories.

1 When reindeer leave the camp, they usually wander around its outskirts. These are places where rubbish is stored.

2 Reindeers move independently from each other at the camp. It is not surprising that the camp is the site of frequent clashes. Camps are full of narrow places, gates and corridors in which animals cannot easily avoid problematic encounters with each other.

3 Any point of constraint of fixity in this environment leaves obvious traces of disruption. The soil around the poles to which reindeer are usually bound for loading is smashed, so no grass grows there.

4 The territory around the camp for hundred meters shows signs of devastation, where reindeer cannot find any food.

5 Sources of concentrated nourishments include dog's feeding pots.

6 The other source of supplementary acids and salts is found in the spots with frozen human urine. In the wild, reindeer can find analogous places beside the trees in which squirrels have nested.

1

2

3

4

7

6

8

6. Comfort

According to reindeer herders the reindeer stay at camp to rest. This state of rest is produced by taking animals out of their environment and building another kind of surrogate environment around them at the camp. At camp there is no grass or moss, no insects (due to the smoke that people provide) and no predators. All the sources of interest and irritation, which form the primary informational environment for reindeer, are excluded. In its place, reindeer receive a small, fenced-off piece of territory devoid of any plants, and small portions of forage and salt. As indicated above, reindeer are left motionless and individualised during their stay at the camp. Reindeer are left in an information blackout, in which the absence of information from the outer world also disorients their communication with each other.

1 Only animals which share common bonds keep close to each other at the camp. This is because the mother remains the primary source of information for the child, through feeding, and vice versa.

2 When there is enough space, animals start to wander around. Their movements are limited and framed by the environment, and are self-contained, in such a way that there is no other goal for these movements than just movement itself. Such autotelic actions are very rare in the lives of reindeer without people.

3 Despite the fact that reindeer herders expect their reindeer to rest at the camp the latter are rarely seen sleeping. It seems that reindeer cannot fall asleep as deeply as people can. They can easily wake up from their dreaming. But at the camp there are few stimuli for them to wake up.

4 Sometimes reindeer are enclosed in tight enclosures where they have to stay very close to each other. This condensation leads to the strange paradox in which animals are fully exposed to each others' messages but do not have information to pass on to each other. This results in a state of alertness in which reindeer spend hours waiting inside the fence.

5 Salt is a very strong stimulant for reindeer, as it is very rare in their environment and is essential for their metabolism. The normal state for them is a lack of salt. But inside the enclosure reindeer experienced the inverse situation – an abundance of salt and absence of other vital substances, usually unlimited in their environment, such as water.

6 Forage is not only a concentration of nutrient elements. It is also distributed in an unnatural manner. For example, it is sprinkled on the ground in lines. Such simple geometric patterns have no precedents in the habitual reindeer environment.

7 The feeding rack also poses a strange task for the reindeer, who never drink all at once from the same river water. Antlers make the accomplishment of such collective eating not only uncomfortable, but also dangerous.

1

2

3

4

5

6

7

8

7. Feeding reindeer

People want to become a comfortable environment for reindeer. Feeding plays an important role in this as it epitomises the idea of a warm relationship – the bond between the feeder and the creature being fed. Feeding is a communicative process in which the search for contact is a primary goal. Reindeer are either attracted by or try to avoid contact with people. People in their turn establish communication with reindeer according to their experience of human communication; when someone makes a gesture of giving food to the animal, the animal's acceptance of the food from human hands is analogous to eye contact in ordinary communication. Reindeer do not always accept the food, and this marks a shift from the mother-child relationship, which people impose by feeding animals, to a flirting relationship, in which people try to seduce animals in order to establish brief contact with them. As a result, people invest emotionally in these situations; not only their warmth and care, but also their wish to be loved and accepted. For the reindeer such moments are more entertaining than nutritionally important. They are especially welcome in the atmosphere of information blackout in which reindeer exist at the camp.

1 Before special procedures such as vaccination or counting the herd, reindeer herders feed and entertain the animals with salt or bread. This is done to establish contact with reindeer, so that further operations go smoothly. This not only makes reindeer look more domestic and cooperative, but also gives people a chance to show that they are not cruel, that they want to be warm and nice to the animals, despite the following rather cruel actions, in which animals are caught, bound, injected, and given medicines.

2 If a reindeer for some reason escapes the fenced enclosure, the first step to catching it is to call and demonstratively offer it food. Usually, however, the escaped animal is too excited to overcome its stress and recognise or accept the offering. Despite its inefficiency, this is the main method of attracting such animals, which speaks for the role that feeding plays – not for animals, but for people that feed them.

3 Feeding animals is fun for children.

4 More experienced herders feed animals without attempting to establish direct contact. Intuitively they prefer to create an atmosphere of abundance and through this communicate with the whole herd, rather than establish personal contact with particular animals.

5 Giving bread to reindeer is an emotionally complex process. Everything starts from the ambivalent disinterest of the man, who at the same time displays that he is eager to distribute bread. His disinterest shows the reindeer that he is not particularly interested in or involved in the situation, which calms the animals and lets them display their own interest.

6 By extension, the reindeer's interest is logically a surprise to the man, although of course this is a pretence, which is experienced as real in this short sequence of the search for contact.

7 When animals begin to accept the food, the man is reserved and does not display his pleasure.

8 Finally, when the animals are encouraged by the first portions of food, the interaction develops into a schismogenetic progression, in which the animals become more and more assertive until all the bread is consumed. The man's passive state in this situation is the inverse of the frame of reindeer herding itself, when people are supposed to actively affect the lives of reindeer.

1

2

3

4

5

6

8. Crush

At the camp reindeer are frequently penned up and stay close to each other. This gives the impression that reindeer form a herd and are more controllable; but this is an illusion. The herd is formed not through the outer boundary that keeps animals together, but by the circulation of messages and feedback loops of these circulations. Animals stay very close to each other only in situations of emergency, when they need to be in proximity to quickly respond to messages from inside. At the camp people unintentionally reconstruct with the help of the fence this particular state of the herd, when animals are in close proximity to each other. As a result the herd is mostly disposed to communication about danger. The paradox is that people initially want the animals to feel peace and absence of danger at the camp, yet place animals in a situation associated with danger and alertness. As a result any movement and change is expected to be the sign of potential danger and people themselves, as the most active and visible inhabitants of the camp, generate the most suspicion.

1 A crush is experienced as a situation in which reindeer do not have enough space to manoeuvre. They cannot stand up without touching and pushing other animals. Every such unintentional contact helps construct a message about the crush. For the herd, being constrained to stay inside the pen is experienced as a situation when instrumental messages, usually sent to maintain their relative proximity and coordination, lose their function and become noise.

2 Outside the pen such messages of proximity help to keep the herd's organisation in transitional moments, for example during crossing a river.

3 When the pen is open, the proximity of animals once again acquires its habitual function and animals go through the gates communicating with each other the same way as they do during crossing a river.

4 When people try to catch animals to count them or administer medicine, the herd once again restores its usual acceptance of proximity as a communicative situation. In such cases the danger that comes from the man inside the pen balances other signals of danger, such as crush itself, and the herd does not suffer from the ambiguous content of the communication. Communication about danger in the pen now has a subject – the real source of danger.

5 In what people assume as panic the reindeer herd behaves in a very organised manner: animals move in a circle, very close to each other forming a kind of swirl.

6 Because the pen is associated with danger, escape is the most logical reaction. Reindeers use every chance to escape through holes in the fence or when they recognise that the posts are not well fixed. Because their behaviour is harmonised and coordinated it is almost impossible to stop them when they do find an opportunity to escape.

1

2

3

4

5

6

7

8

9. Gates

The gate is a point of access in a line of impassibility. And in this respect gates are informative for a herd. They are so remarkable that the herd almost cannot avoid the seduction of passing through a gate, or any hole in the fence that serves as a gate. If one animal finds a point to escape, all other animals follow. This happens partly because the hole in the fence is an easy solution of the problem of where to go, it immediately constitutes a focus for the herd. In this respect when people build fences in the forest to enclose reindeer in valleys. At the same time as encircling them with these enormous constructions, they inevitably also construct gaps through which the reindeer can escape; no fence can be maintained without a hole appearing somewhere along the line. The fences that people build do not have special gateways, and a gate can be made an unmade anywhere just by pulling out the horizontal rails and then re-inserting them. The appearance of holes in fences is inevitable, but where these gaps occur is an open question. For the herd, because its whole movement and navigation is coordinated by the pattern of reading a landscape to establish where to go, gaps in fences are informative keys and as a result they find them more easily than people. People construct fences to enclose the reindeer, but from the perspective of the herd, people actually construct gaps, which mark their way through. Without the fence there would be no obsession with escape, although of course it does not mean that the animals would stay in the valleys where people want them to live.

1 Gates are not seen as way in or out, but as a narrow channel by which to proceed further. The herd enters a gate one by one following the man with forage without suspicion that this is the way into a pen.

2 Driving reindeer inside a pen can be done by attracting them to follow, or driving them off. In the first case people give information about the food that awaits reindeer in the pen, they become part of the herd – their movements are accommodated by the herd as if they are one of its members. When people drive reindeer off, they present themselves as an outside danger.

3 When reindeer leave the pen people once again act as a danger and can direct the herd to go in a particular direction from the pen by cutting off the direction they do not want the herd to take.

4 Also, when the herd leaves the pen, people can count the reindeer, as the animals go through the narrow gates one by one. When counting, people are relatively passive observers. This is not different when people walk in front of the herd or follow it driving it into the pen. It is difficult to count reindeer inside the pen, because at least some animals are constantly and chaotically on the move. The only number that herders can obtain – is the number of reindeer leaving the camp. As the animals go into the forest this number is no longer valid, because some animals can run away from the herd.

5 Sometimes part of the herd remains enclosed in the pen and the other part is driven to the camp to reunite the whole herd. At this point the opened gate is a sign to go through for all animals. Potentially this is a situation in which the first part of the herd can escape.

6 Then people have to switch to the message of danger, as this message is less contextual and more abstract. Both parts of the herd would respond to threatening calls and movements, while only those who were driven from the forest would be interested in forage. And those who stayed inside the pen would be more attracted by the possibility of escaping than of eating forage they have already received.

7 To exclude the risk of a herd escaping through the gates people prefer not to make gates for themselves to get in and out of the pen. Instead they squeeze through without pulling off the horizontal rails.

8 In winter, when reindeer are much more dependent on human sources of salt people can keep the pen open and reindeer freely walk around the camp going in and out of the pen. These are very rare moments, when people do not have to intrude into the communicative organisation of the herd to make it stay at the camp for any length of time.

1

2

3

4

5

6

7

8

10. Catching reindeer

Sometimes people need to catch a reindeer inside the pen to conduct medical observation or vaccinate it. This moment of catching is a point of transformation of the relationship between the man and the animal. The animal, when it is caught, is separated from the herd not spatially but communicatively, it cannot freely react to messages from the herd and the content of its own messages to the herd is reduced to a signal of danger. Whereas a reindeer will continue to avoid and resist contact even when caught, people anticipate the result – a catch, and respond accordingly. Even when it has been caught, this for the reindeer implies no clear change of situation because it continues to resist. This means that what for reindeer is a continuous situation of various signals and messages entails for people a switch of activities, because after the animal is caught, people have to hold it and conduct the intended procedure. The moment of capture experienced by people and animals in different frames is a moment of physical contact. For people this contact is a purpose that transforms into a condition enabling further planned actions. For animals this contact is a moment of transcendental fear, when the animal does not need any additional information to react, it just resists as strongly as it can. This simple attitude affects the whole process when people and the animal become one communicative system. The resistance of the animal always threatens the pre-planned course of people's actions. People can never be certain that the catch was successful until they have finished all their tasks and released the animal. So even if people hold animals, to some extent they continue to catch them until the moment of release. The most effective strategy is to catch the animal unexpectedly, but this unexpectedness remains intrinsic to the situation for both parties, because the animal can in the same way unexpectedly escape.

1 An unexpected catch is the only option, when animals are not penned up and can ran away and disperse. There can only be one attempt, because the reindeer will expect the second one.

2 In the pen, reindeer run in a circle when people try to catch them. This makes it much more difficult, because people have not only to follow the reindeer they want to catch, but also cross other reindeers that run close to it.

3-4 When people catch a reindeer, their actions are harmonised with each other through their focus on the same body. When the animal escapes, people stay in this synchronicity for some time after the failed attempt.

5 Sometimes the herder does not know whether he caught the animal or not, only after a series of phases of resistance and tension through which both the animal and the herder should pass can the herder feel that the animal (and discover which animal) is caught. These sequences could be compared with calibration in the process of joining into one system.

6 When the noose reaches an antler, it is loose and the reaction and resistance of the animal is needed to tighten it up. Usually this happens so fast that it is not clear which set of antlers from the rushing herd have been caught.

7 Because everything happens very fast the herder has to be prepared to draw the rope immediately after it is stretched between the antler and his hand. This is felt far earlier than it can be seen.

8 After the noose has been tightened, the herder pulls the animal towards himself until he can reach the antlers and hold them. The animal resists, but it is already a part of the human-reindeer system, and every pull of the animal is felt through the rope and can be counterbalanced by the man – also through the rope.

1

2

3

4

5

6

7

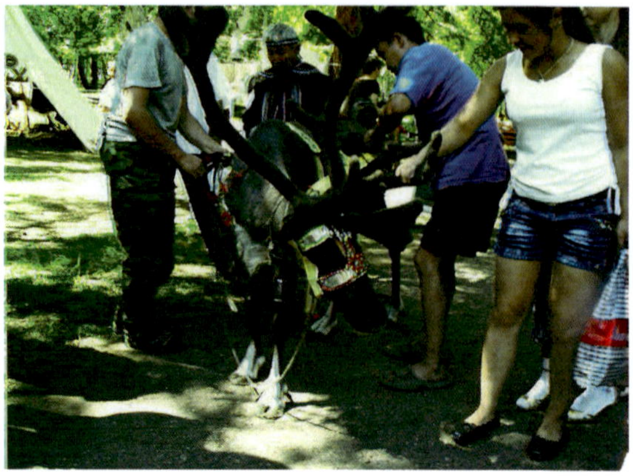

8

11. Holding an animal's body

Because people are not responsive to the messages of the reindeer the only way for them to become one communicative system with the animal is through the violence, when the animal's body and its reactions become the point to which people are connected, trying to hold and suppress it. To hold an animal people have to react to its reactions. And because the source of this resistance goes from one organism and various forms of it are interconnected, the people that gather around the animal become interconnected with each other through their individual reactions to the reactions of the animal. The multiplicity of the work of muscles of different parts of the body and their potential strength embrace several people into one unity: the group that catches the reindeer. People become extensions of the reindeer's body, of the parts that they hold, and their actions are coordinated not through a common cooperative strategy but by individual reactions to the coordinated resistance and struggle of the animal's body. This form of sociality can be labelled 'companionship', when people react to a situation collectively performing individual tasks that are distributed not according to rules or previous arrangements, but according to a person's unique involvement into the situation. Every person reacts to the partial piece of the total situation that is available to him or her. The distribution of these pieces of experience can be rather random, but because they all are parts of a single system that generates them, they all carry common patterns. People that are connected to each other through their individual and partial reactions to the same totality (i.e. a system) form a communicative system that appropriates the patterns of the system to which they are.

1 The anatomy of the animal engenders the logic according to which people catch the animal. They start from the less flexible parts such as antlers, and then proceed to the more and more flexible ones. The first person that grabs the animal holds the antlers. The animal can respond with its most intensive strength, but in its response it positions itself in one direction – opposed to the person the holds the antlers.

2 Then other people come, they grab a tail, feet, the neck of the animal. Then the animal cannot resist without hurting itself.

3 The more the animal persists in seeking a concrete direction of escape, the more confusion it experiences, as people attack from various sides simultaneously.

4 Finally people surround the animal like a living fence, inside which the animal is fixed. But it is fixed not because it is bound or suppressed only by strength. It is bound because its body parts are twisted and the coordination between them is broken. People intrude and create contradictions in the relationships between the parts of its body.

5 Large and strong animals require a lot more people to suppress them. A bull, example, can be caught only if three people start by holding his antlers.

6 People also exclude and disable some of the most functional parts of the animal. For example, by twisting a leg so that the animal cannot walk away.

7 A big animal cannot be fenced by people, but has to be thrown down on the ground, so that people can press the animal with their bodyweight. To run away the animal has not only to resist people's efforts, but also to overcome gravity.

8 At public feasts when reindeer are used as live decorations the audience also explores the body of the animal according to the same logic. People mostly touch the antlers, and sometimes the back and neck. The animal is usually trapped, tethered by a rope to the tree, for example.

1

2

3

4

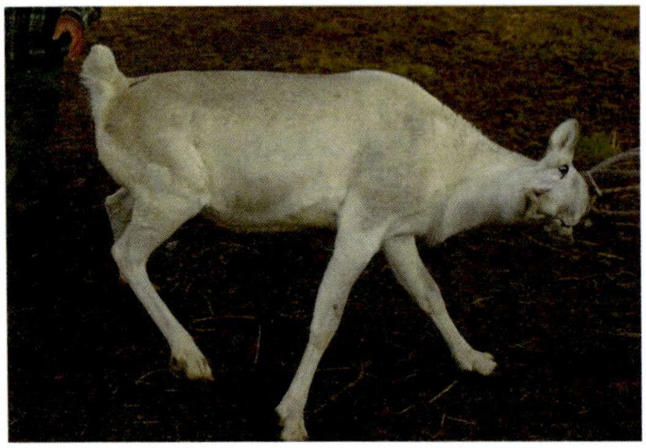
5

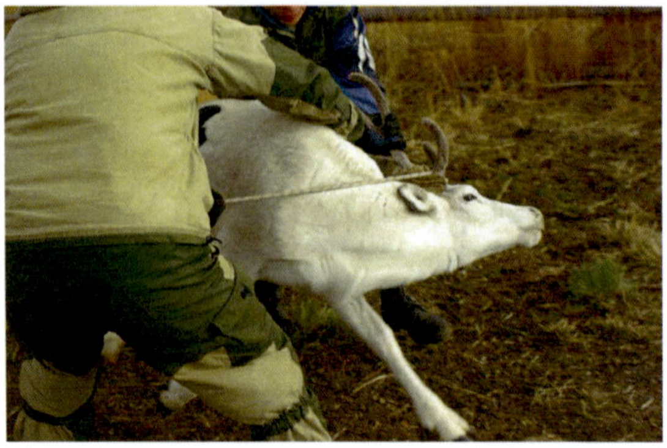
6

7

8

12. Dragging an animal with a rope

Dragging a reindeer with a rope helps to prevent many risks, such as the risk of injury from antlers. At the same time this needs more men. But because the whole process happens across only one axis that connects people and the animal, it is much more predictable. People have to control only this one tension and do not have to anticipate any unexpected movements of the animal. The animal is involved in its resistance and because it is focused on one point, it is predictable and controllable. Rope provides safety for people, it mediates physical contact, and both people and reindeer find the situation less traumatic. But exactly because there is less risk of injury, some people behave much more aggressively than when they catch animals without a rope. People and animals are not so tightly attached to each other in the frames of this scheme of catching. The freedom of action that people receive is a freedom to dominate. And not all of them can resist the opportunity to perform their situated domination. But exactly this bias in the animal-reindeer relationship causes problems at the moment of release, when people have to once again reach the animal physically to untie the noose. This is a very dangerous moment, when the angry animal can butt or kick the previously dominant men.

1 One of the most effective strategies is to drag the animal towards another pen and to open the gate between pens only to transfer the animal. The gate should be closed after the animal so as to prevent other animals from running through. The dragged animal is released only after the gate is closed, in order not to let it ran back. All this is done when people have to be sure that they don't catch animals twice and give a double dose of vaccine, or if they need to count the animals one by one.

2 The rope is like the locks in a canal. Each man that holds the rope forms a lock, which can be opened, if the man lets go off the rope. In this system like in the locks of a canal, one lock should always be closed, otherwise the animal will run away (like the water from an open sluice gate).

3 Four men drag the animal through an open gate. This needs additional effort, because men have to define the direction in which to drag a struggling animal and not just respond chaotically to the animal. There interaction should be channelled through the gate. This is not only dragging, but also navigation.

4 This is the moment, when dragging men need assistance from another man who can push the animal into the right direction. The animal has no opportunity to respond to this push, because all its efforts are concentrated on resisting the rope.

5 When an animal pulls the rope over, its movements are fixed along one axis. When the animal feels that its strength is insufficient, it tries to reconfigure its resistance. But it cannot change the axis of resistance. The only manoeuvre left to it is to rotate around on the axis, for example, to twist its head.

6 To release the animal people have to hold its body. This is the moment, when direct physical contact between the reindeer and men is restored. And this is the most dangerous moment in the situation.

7 Sometimes people switch between dragging the rope and holding parts of the animal's body. This happens if people need to tether the animal to milk it, administer a vaccine or conduct an observation. When people hold the animal, no one is dragging, but the rope stays attached to antlers, so that it can be dragged immediately after the procedure is finished. To continue dragging is dangerous, because if the animal is given one particular point to resist it will hurt other people. Holding the animal is effective only if people manage to distribute the pressure on the animal across its different parts. The rope provides a focus that prevents this distribution and confusion.

8 At the moment of release people are exposed to danger, because after the rope is released they cease to be a united system of locks with a cumulative effect. After the rope is released men are individuals. And every individual man is weaker than the individual reindeer, equipped with antlers and strong legs.

1

2

3

4

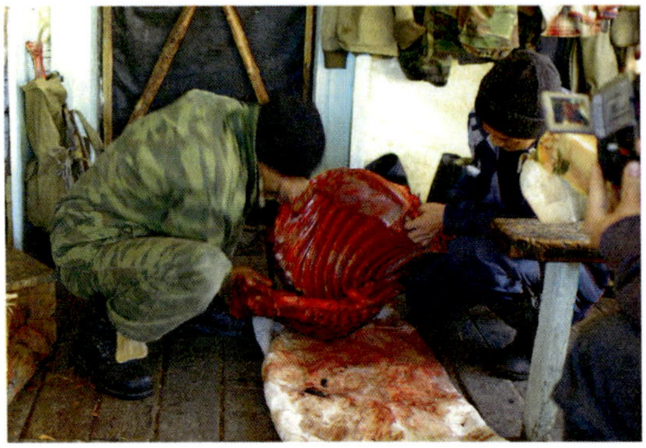
5

6

7

8

13. Parts of reindeer: meat

When an animal is separated from the herd, it loses its ability to communicate directly with the herd and participate in the transmission of self-correcting messages. To separate the animal is to make a first step toward its death. But death is not the end of the process of separation. A reindeer's meat is chopped into pieces, separated from the carcass and then reassembled again for storage. Then it is distributed and pieces of this meat go in different directions, to other taiga camps, to the village, to the regional centre and other places. All along their way these pieces of meat collect people. Meat attracts neighbours and relatives, friends and colleagues. When cooked, the meat is once again chopped into smaller pieces to be boiled or fried, and then distributed among the guests of a feast. The death of the reindeer starts with separation and then it carries the potential to balance this initial separation by reuniting and gathering together people that consume its meat. The animal that is taken out of the communicative web of its herd becomes a reason for people to interact and maintain their own communicative web. The disassembled parts of the body attract and assemble people. When people want to secure their solitude and avoid contact with others, they have to hide the meat, collect all its pieces together and cover it, as if to reassemble the body once again.

1 After the kill, butchering starts with skinning, so that animal does not look like a homogeneous organism, but uncovered shows its anatomy as interconnected parts.

2 Butchering is a process of careful separation of organs. People disassemble the body, separating the inner organs, sorting and displaying them as detached parts.

3 For storage, because the body is too big to transport all its parts in one round, people build a special construction with a so-called 'table' on poles. Here they store all the disassembled organs and parts and cover them with the skin. This simulation of reassembly is done to prevent other animals and birds from gathering around the body to have their own feast.

4 To transport it, the parts of the body are once again reassembled, to fit the volume of the bags.

5 The first persons attracted by news about the meat return to the camp. The people that gather at the camp, cut the meat into pieces to transport it further from the taiga to village and city. This assembling of people is paralleled by a disassembling of the reindeer's body.

6 And once again, before departing in different directions, people collect all the left meat and store it all together in a box, where it will stay frozen outdoors until the next occasion of sharing. The separation of people corresponds to the collection of the meat parts together.

7 Only at the camp during preparations for its transport (actually, at the precise moment of sharing) meat is displayed uncovered like during the first phases of butchering.

8 When stored or transported meat is usually covered. When individuals with meat go on their way, the meat is not on display, partly because its sight will attract other people. Only if they know that they will cross nobody along their path do people transport meat openly. But this is done only to reassemble it later and cover it, when entering territories where contact with other people is unavoidable.

1

2

3

4

5

6

7

14. Parts of reindeer: skin

Reindeer hides go through a process of being cut into pieces and then reconstituted as a patchwork during which they are reassembled according to a new aesthetic logic. The skin that previously covered the shape of the body in three-dimensional space is cleaned and flattened. The individual qualities of every animal – the colour of its fur, its length and texture – are now seen as materials for creating patterns in which pieces from one hide are mixed with the pieces of other hides. Through patchwork, an initially singular quality becomes the basis for repetitive patterns, which form an aesthetically appealing fur mosaic ornament that Evenki people call kumalans. These mosaics frequently become gifts that people send to each other as reminders of their relationships. For example, a daughter gives it to her parents with whom she no longer lives. Pieces for kumalan are cut out of reindeer hide to fit together with pieces from the skins of other species (sables, lynxes and so forth). To make the ornament interesting the master needs various skins, which are collected from different hunters. In the process of creating kumalans reindeer herding is combined with all sorts of things such as hunting and hunters, mostly female stitchers, the children who help, tourists that buy them as souvenirs, etc. The skin was the visible part of the animal; used to create kumalans it makes Evenki people visible to other ethnic groups, as it becomes a symbol that represents them.

1 The hide of the reindeer, except the parts that covered legs, is left in the forest. It is hanged to attract birds to eat the leftovers of the meat.

2 The skin that covered its legs is cleaned the night after the skinning. These parts will be used to make fur boots. What recently covered the legs of a reindeer, will warm people's feet.

3 Cut and cleaned skins are left drying attached by nails to the walls of the camp house.

4 The skins from the faces of young reindeer that died in wolf attacks soon after they were born are frequently used as bedding to sit on.

5 One of the most famous kumalans in the region, displayed at the local museum. The other one was sent as a present to the president of Russia.

6 Mother and son demonstrate their skills in sewing kumalans at the ethnic fair in the centre of the region.

7 Different kumalans are assembled together at the ethnic fair. They form a patchwork of patchworks. This repeats the pattern that forms the motif of the fair itself: to represent different groups of local Evenki as one ethnic group.

1

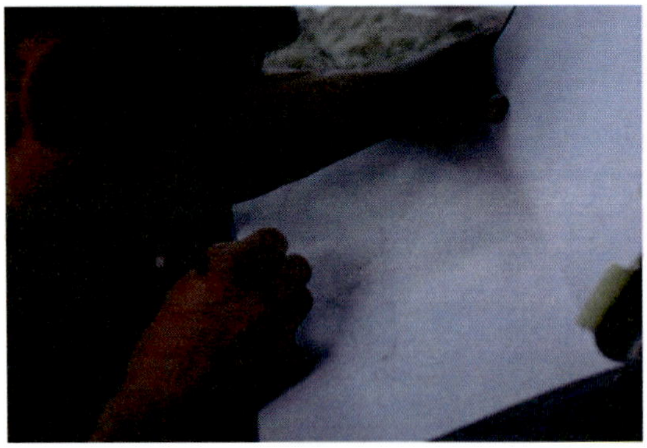

2

3

4

5

6

7

15. Parts of reindeer: images

Pictures and photos of reindeer are special trophies because they conserve the image of an animal that is no longer alive. A picture freezes a moment of coherence, when parts of the reindeer were integrated with each other. Such pictures show life; notably they show a pattern of relationships between elements. These elements could be stored as objects – such as antlers –, but photos conserve not the object, but the relationships in which the antlers were embedded when the reindeer that had them and was alive. People pictured with animals are also embedded into this situated context of relatedness and cohesion. That is one of the reasons, why people like to be photographed with reindeer. Such photos depict them as being in relationship (at least by proxy) with life. This impression is created precisely because when a photo is looked at, the depicted reindeer is most probably dead. This high probability is the result of the trajectory of the animal, having been selected and separated from the herd. As noted above, separation from the herd is the beginning of death. As a result a photo with a reindeer depicts a moment when the animal is yet alive, but the photo itself tells us that this animal is not alive anymore. This ambiguity of death and life, with their temporalities overlapping, makes such photos enigmatic and impressive. People gather together to take such photos and they gather again and again to look at them.

1 At the ethnic fair the reindeer was the main feature of the Evenki section of the exhibition. Later it was killed, cooked and eaten by members of the Evenki delegation and their guests.

2 Drawings of reindeer depict the most picturesque and violent moments of a reindeer's life. For example, they show how reindeer struggle with each other during the rutting season.

3 Images created by craft are usually more static than drawings or photography. In photography exposure and aperture must correspond with the speed of action in any given image. In drawings dynamic scenes are often depicted with dynamic strokes. On the other hand static portraits of reindeer are carved with slow and accurate movements of the knife.

4 To be photographed with a kumalan is similar to being portrayed with a reindeer. A kumalan is an assemblage of elements that depicts an aesthetic pattern, which corresponds to the experience of perception of the overall pattern present in live organisms.

5 The man with a reindeer is a powerful image, and it is the dominant icon in depictions of Evenki people. Ethnographic films about reindeer herders are inevitably advertised with this image. Such advertisements attract people to gather together and watch the film, just as photos with reindeer collect people to look at them.

6-7 The prototypes of these canonical advertisements are kept in the family archives of reindeer herders.

1

2

3

4

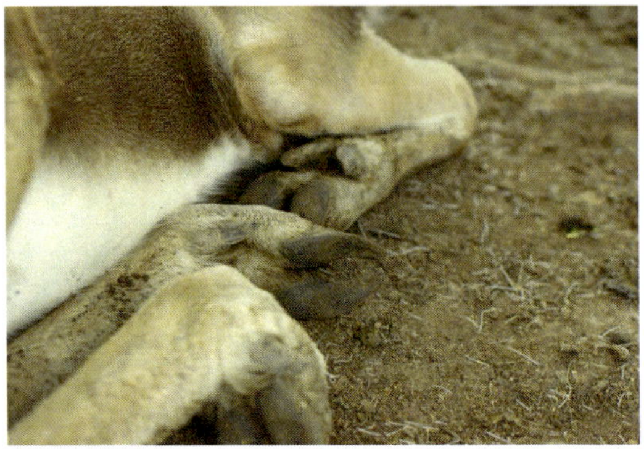
5

6

16. Death

During our stay with reindeer herders we took a number of photographs with reindeer that our hosts categorically disliked. We were taking photographs of reindeer from inside the pen. So constrained, we could only take photographs from a very short distance. Playing with this possibility we made photos not of animals as a whole, but of their parts. When we showed these experimental images to the herders, they did not like them. There was no explanation of this, but the images disturbed them and they refused to look at these photographs again. The striking parallels with other photographs that we took during our fieldwork gave us a clue to understanding this reaction. Despite the fact that we were recording live animals in our experimental photos, we did not try to depict them as whole organisms. These photos constituted attempts to visually separate the parts of the animal from its body. This separation created an atmosphere of death also transmitted by other photographs that we took, of parts of the dead animal after the butchering. People found pictures of reindeer attractive when they depicted as alive animals that were now dead. These pictures preserve lives now past, and as such they are charged with and radiate the spirit of life. But pictures that depict living animals as dead, decomposed into parts, do the opposite: they show death.

1 This photo is taken with a 50mm fixed lens inside the pen. It would not possible to take a picture of the head with antlers, without other parts of the animal outside the pen because it would be almost impossible to get close enough to the animal to observe it remaining motionless.

2 During butchering the head and antlers are cut from the rest of the body and it is the last part to be skinned.

3 The position of this tail shows that the animal is calm, but not happy.

4 The fur of the tail is burnt on an open fire. The tail without its fur is then stored in a dry place to sell to Chinese buyers that use it to prepare a traditional medicine.

5 The position of the legs of the animal at rest.

6 The legs of a reindeer after being skinned. The skin from the legs is used to make fur boots.

1

2

3

4

6

5

7

1. New means of transport

Being nomads, the Evenki are very interested in every possible means of movement and traveling. New transportation creates the possibility to move faster and to carry more things. These new capacities change the world of the Evenki because, as they are able to carry more with them, they can possess more in general. And if they have more things, it makes their life more stable, localized and less nomadic. New types of transport bring new kinds of dependencies upon the outside world. The other aspect of this dependency is the fact that new transportation is neither capable of crossing great distances in the taiga, nor is it cheap to exploit independently. So most of the expensive means of transport are controlled by outsiders and the Evenki cannot use them in their own interests. Older forms of transportation, such as reindeer and horses, are still kept by the Evenki, although they are not used as extensively as they were prior to the integration of cars, all-terrain vehicles and tractors. But until such times as these new means of transport are totally controlled by the Evenki, their life in the taiga remains impossible without horses and reindeers.

1 Chinese wheeled tractors, specialized in nephrite mining, have been bought by the local Evenki community, and given to several Evenki families. These are mainly used to carry tree trunks from the forest to the camp. Winter is the only season when these machines do not stick in the mud.

2-3 Old all-terrain track type vehicles are bought from military camps by the same Evenki community and are mainly used to transport nephrite from the mine to the city. The Evenki travel with these vehicles when they go deep into the taiga to work there as hunters for the community. Every week several such vehicles stop at the Evenki reindeer camp situated half way between the nephrite mine and the last village. Here the drivers and the security have a short rest. The majority of the food supply of the reindeer camp is transported also by these all-terrain vehicles.

4 It is only possible to use vehicles such as the Chinese tractors in winter and only along the frozen rivers, which in winter look like polished highways.

5 Horses are still the most popular form of transport. They are even preferred by the reindeer herders who use them to transport things between the summer and the winter camps. However, they need all-terrain vehicles for the main seasonal removal, because horses cannot carry all of their bulky and heavy possessions. But horses are indispensable in hunting.

6 Reindeer are now very rarely used, but there are still places, where they are the only form of transport for the Evenki. People do not ride them anymore, which makes traveling with them less convenient. People have become taller and the reindeer have become smaller.

7 Airplanes still fly to the isolated villages of the region, but the tickets are too expensive. Ordinary flights are rare because there are seldom enough passengers willing to buy tickets. But medical emergency flights take place and local residents always try to take advantage of the opportunity to fly with these airplanes for free.

1

2

3

4

5

6

7

2. Combination of new technologies with each other

The introduction of any new technology brings about such changes in the amounts and quality of task accomplishments that it is impossible to combine such technology with older technologies with lower capacities. Usually new devices are connected to each other, so one thing changes the whole spectrum of various tasks, and creates a need to introduce other new technical equipment. Without combination with other new equipment, these innovations are excluded from the existing web of older technologies, and cannot be integrated into everyday life at all.

1-2 The use of petrol-powered saws makes no sense without a tractor, because of the amount of trees that can be cut down and then need to be transported to the camp. Usually, with such saws, people cut more than they did before and, as a result, they need to go deeper into the forest for new trees of the required quality. Longer distances and greater amounts of tree trunks determine the need for a tractor.

3-4 All-terrain vehicles have brought with them the possibility of various new forms of hunting. For example the hunter can travel at night and use lights to find wild animals. Paralyzed by the light beam in the night, animals are not able to run away. They run along the track of the beam because they can see only those parts of the terrain that are lighted. It is very easy to kill such helpless creatures. But the use of lights at night is impossible to combine with traditional hunting transport such as horses. Horses do not work well at night and you cannot bring the power supply for the lamp with them. And even in the event of success, the hunter won't be able to transport all the meat, because usually hunting with lights provides the opportunity to kill several animals during one night. In picture 3 the hunters are constructing a lamp that can be operated manually. Picture 4 shows a hatch in the roof of the vehicle, through which the standing hunter can use the lamp and then shoot the animals that are caught in its beam..

5-7 Binoculars are not absolutely a new thing for the Evenki. They have used them ever since they acquired guns with a longer shooting range. New guns have even longer range, and they are supplied with telescopic sights. This is important, because animals that are seen from a longer distance need less time to escape, and the hunter has less time to switch from the binoculars to the gun sight in which he needs to find the animal once again. These two technologies, connected with seeing and shooting, always predetermine each other.

1

2

3

4

5

6

7

8

3. Parallel old and new technologies I

Although new technical devices are generally not compatible with old ones, they do not supplant old technologies at all. Old ones may be less productive, but they are much more reliable, and so they continue to be maintained as reserve options, which are important in the frequent cases of emergency, when new devices break down or there is no petrol for their function. Life in the taiga and isolated villages predetermines such episodes of crisis for new technologies, which can only be fixed or supplied through contact with the outside world, and this contact is not possible for extended periods of time. At the same time the introduction of new technologies presupposes the support of older parallel ones, even if these older ones were already out of practice and nearly forgotten. In this process the progress of technology goes hand-in-hand with the reminiscence of older, more conservative elements of culture. As a result only those new technologies persist, which have parallel options from the traditional repertoire of Evenki culture. Even though the practical accomplishment of everyday tasks changes and develops, the general cultural matrix of everyday tasks remain the same.

1-4 Evenings allow time for leisure and relaxation. Watching films has become an ordinary evening practice, which in the event of the failure of a diesel generator can be replaced by reading books and journals. And here the oil lamp helps to resolve the problem of lighting. Picture 3 shows one of three diesel generators that belong to an Evenki family living at a reindeer camp. Sometime even all three of them are out of commission, or there is not enough fuel to start them up. Sometimes the Evenki travel to nearby winter huts for hunting, where they are not able to take diesel generators with them. In both these cases oil lamps are used in the evenings.

5-6 At the reindeer camp the Evenki use a water pump installed in an adjacent river, which is supplied with energy by a diesel generator. However in an isolated village the Evenki need to carry water themselves, in buckets ad other containers because the river is too far away from the house. At a reindeer camp deep in taiga the Evenki even keep a small garden, which they water using these utensils. But the products from this garden do not play a crucial role in their diet and the Evenki do not depend upon or too care much about it. The pump makes their life easier, but they always maintain the possibility of carrying water themselves.

7-8 In an isolated village the only way to be connected with people from other villages is to use a satellite phone, which is installed in the local administration building This telephone uses Russian satellites which are not very reliable, so the signal is frequently too weak to establish connection. The telephone needs electricity which is supplied only at certain hours, when the village diesel generator is working. People are accustomed to this instability of phone connection and use it more as an entertainment, than as a regular communication facility. In a distant reindeer camp, where there is no satellite phone and people live for longer than half the year without any news from their relatives, they use alternative ways of connecting with them, such as divination and the reading of cards.

1

2

3

4

5

6

4. Parallel old and new technologies II

All old technologies once were new. Over time, as they become more and more inevitably embedded into everyday practice, the type of coordination of activities of different parties involved in them slowly changes from complementary to symmetrical mode. This means that slowly all people learn how to use the technology and the position of a specialist and introductory sponsor is eliminated. At the same time, the growing dependency on the products of the technology requires the mobilization of the forces of all members of the community equally. The parallel coexistence of new and old technologies also plays a role in maintaining the balance between complementary and symmetrical relationships between people. Situations of affluence and comfort associated with a complementary mode of actions are counterbalanced by emergencies, when symmetry is the only way to mobilize all members to overcome difficulties.

1-2 One person is operating a petrol-powered saw, while the other person is directing the fall of the tree. The new technology has predetermined such a complementary distinction between the roles of the involved actors. The two-handed manual saw needs the equal force and involvement of two persons, and the cutting is not so fast that people cannot at the same time direct the falling of the tree. Their involvement in the task is symmetrical.

3-6 Either a tractor or an all-terrain vehicle is driven by one person, while the other acts as navigator, steering a safe passage between the trees, or checking that the trunks are stoutly bound together. The transportation of the trunks without vehicles needs the work of all members, both men and women. In Picture 4 the figure of a woman stands a little aside watching as men drag the sledge laden with trunks out of a gully in the snow, but in the next moment she seizes one trunk, puts it on her shoulders, and carries it the whole way home like others. She also carries an axe.

1

2

3

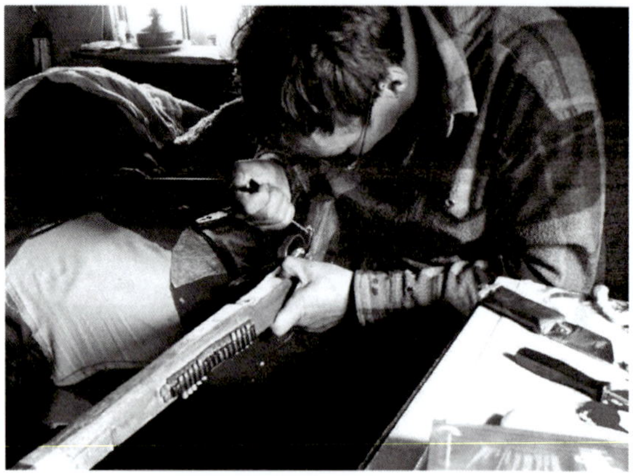
4

5

6

7

8

5. Repairing technical devicesl

Repairing is a task in its own right that is more frequently connected with just passing the time or simple curiosity, than with the practical setting-up of a device. If something is easily broken and too complex to be repaired over the course of an evening, it is usually dropped from the set of equipment in active regular use within the household, and for years can become a focus of the owner's curiosity and attempts to repair it, without any apparent regret that it is not working anymore. This practice becomes a part of a special kind of leisure. Repair is also a step in the process of sorting out, when unreliable and fragile new technologies are rejected. The Evenki rarely discard things, they prefer to combine them, and to explore all new and possible options. From this point of view, repairing a thing is one way not to openly exclude it by throwing it away, but to find it a new function within the household, at the very least to make it a toy to be played with in leisure time. For this reason the Evenki do not try to systematically understand the device and its workings, but simply attempt various combinations of actions, hoping for the chance that somehow it will work. As a result these manipulations more often than not lead to the definitive destruction of a mechanism. Knowing this, certain persons in the household, for whom the function of the device is somehow important, prevent all the attempts of others to repair it, trying to save it in its original form before seeking external assistance from the outside world.

1-2 Anytime that Semka was free, in the evening or daytime, he would try to repair a radio that originally would have been powered by a compact solar battery. The wires were so mixed up and cut at several places, that it was obvious that Semka was clearly not the first person to attempt to repair it. Yet still Semka persisted and did not abandon the task, and came back to the radio from time to time.

3 In this picture Nikolai Stepanovich is trying to fix a car, which he managed to doom this occasion. However, later on, it broke down whilst being driven very far from home and had to be left where it was. The fate of the car is unknown to us.

4 Sometimes assembling something from various parts, taking care and repairing is all part of the same process, endless and embedded into the practice of usage. This is especially true for illegal devices, such as uncertified guns, which it is not possible to obtain and repair openly. Practically, these semi-broken things are usually deployed as alternatives to normal mainstream things, but they take a lot of time and attention from their owners.

5-6 Machines that need starting up (such as tractors or generators) are always at risk, because any unsuccessful attempt to start them up can initiate a consequent attempt to repair them.

7-8 If some device is not easily repaired and the possible various combinations of obvious actions have been tried without success, then usually the Evenki try to resolve the problem by force. This also usually leads to additional breakdowns.

1

2

3

4

5

6

6. New visual technologies

Leisure as a sphere that is not connected with survival and its production contains less risky situations and fewer potential emergencies; consequently, it provides more options for the integration of new and experimental technologies. Modern leisure technologies are mainly represented by various visual devices, such as televisions, computers and cameras. This sphere is dominated by play as a mode of action; in particular, it attracts children. Although these technologies do not depend so much on parallel old technologies to find a place in the Evenki ecology of tasks, their position is also not stable. Largely this is because all new modern visual technologies presuppose intense and constant connection with the internet, or with television frequencies, or with mobile telephone frequencies, or with program upgrades. The isolated Evenki life with its incidental contacts with outsiders does not provide such stable interconnections. Hence, the only new visual technologies, associated with leisure, which find their place in Evenki life, are those which presuppose only accidental contacts with the outside world. And very few modern visual technologies meet such criteria.

1 Children combine their playing with toys and watching television like adults combine various technologies and tasks with each other.

2 A lively party is frequently accompanied by a switched-on TV, which is usually watched by children who are excluded from the adults' feasts. At the same time its noise creates an atmosphere of revelry.

3 In the computer games that Maxim is playing he is firing in virtual reality. In his real life at reindeer camp he has his own gun and is learning to shoot at targets. He is preparing to become a hunter like his father. The computer that he plays with in the village is at risk, because it can easily be infiltrated by viruses. Anti-viruses programs do not help much, because there is no connection to the internet to upgrade their data bases.

4 The Evenki have to repeatedly watch the same films, in their DVD collection, because they can't install a satellite antenna. Even if they had one, they have no access to a specialist with the expertise to be able to properly orient it to work at their distant reindeer camp.

5-6 Showing photos is a common practice when receiving guests. But the Evenki like to view them from time to time themselves. The photos they collect represent mainly the history of their contacts with other people. They can't print the photos they would like to, and are restricted to only those that are given to them by visiting outsiders.

1

2

3

4

5

6

7. Integration of new technologies

The Evenki are simultaneously curious and very pragmatic. They are interested in how new things can be used and are open to all the new possibilities that new technologies bring. When a new technical device appears, firstly they try to integrate it into existing schemes of technology. If the device fits into the preexisting niche, it frequently maintains this concrete function in the Evenki household. Consequently, new technologies are adjusted to the Evenki way of life and change it more in quantitative scale rather than in qualitative.

1-2 Andrei is playing with our video camera. He has accommodated it very quickly to the habitual practice of seeing through binoculars.

3 Binoculars are a common instrument, which Andrei uses when searching for reindeer.

4 Maxim also found the same function of the camera without our assistance. He also liked the zoom function, which resembled the telescopic sight of the gun that is used by his father.

5-6 Looking at the world through an artificial sight is a common experience shared both by women and men. The adjustment of a gun also presupposes several attempts at searching through a sight before firing.

1

2

3

4

5

6

1. Nephrite road

Nephrite is a precious stone that local people extract from the open cast mine and sell to Chinese buyers. The mine is situated deep in the forest far from settlements on lands that previously were used by Evenki reindeer herders and hunters. Alongside the Evenki community, local Russian, Buryat and Chinese people participate in extracting the nephrite. Nephrite is transported during the whole summer season from May to October on a weekly basis. Caravans of all-terrain vehicles pass through several stations that belong to the community. These stations, with all their buildings, instruments and storages, as well as tracks and all-terrain vehicles, constitute the infrastructure of the nephrite road. The stone flows along this channel, and substantial parts of the profits from its sale are spent to maintain the channel. If we think of the nephrite road as a channel, and the nephrite as a message to be delivered from the place of its origin to the Chinese buyers who send it further on to the market, then we also can see this channel as a noise, through which the message passes. The infrastructure of the nephrite road is created and maintained by people, it is distinct from the wild natural background. Without people, who connect various flows of supplies, petrol and stone, with their own work, nephrite would not even exist as a separate thing. It would stay as a part of the mountain, concrete and covered with soil and trees.

1 The nephrite mountain is dynamited. Pieces of nephrite lie in piles and people extract the biggest pieces they can move to be transported.

2 The selected rocks are stored on the wooden platform, high enough to make the process of loading the all-terrain vehicle easier.

3 Because they do not need a road, all-terrain vehicles are the only transport that can go through the forests and rivers that lie between the mine and the closest village. At the same time such vehicles consume enormous quantities of petrol.

4 There are several stations where the caravan stops before reaching the last point. At some of these stations people eat and rest, at other stations they can fix breakdowns and fill tanks with petrol.

5 On its way to the city nephrite is reloaded several times from one means of transport to another.

6 Nephrite is a white stone that is very precious in China. In Russia this stone does not have any special value. On the Chinese market the pieces from this deposit can be sold for relatively cheap craftwork or to be used as a material for making replicas of authentic objects meant to be from ancient China. The nephrite road or the channel for the nephrite flow is a way the stone is delivered from the context where it has almost no value to the context in which it can be very precious. The message carried by the stone along the nephrite road is this difference.

1

2

3

4

5

6

2. Stations

On its way from the mine to the town, where it will be sold, the nephrite passes through several stations of various degrees of autonomy and complexity of organization. At some points the stone is reloaded from one means of transport onto the other, at other points, passing through stations does not affect the stone at all. At some places people can have rest and get food, at other places they can fix technical problems, check the engines of the transport and fill up tanks with petrol. Spaces between the stations are spaces of exhaustion – where people and engines get tired and break down. Stations are points at which to cool down the engines and get rest. Stations also mark the route. They break it into 4 - 6 hour runs that help to control and reduce overwork of both people and vehicles. The nephrite is accompanied by various other elements on its way, but only the nephrite goes through all of the stations from the original post to the last point of selling. With one exception: there is one person who accompanies the nephrite along the whole route. This person has worked on this route for several years and we can say that everything, even the nephrite, is interchangeable, but not this one man. We propose to see this as an attempt to assure the humanistic component of the nephrite road project. People impose and strengthen their presence in the phenomenon that is to such an extent fixed on the mineral. The capacity of the channel is now constrained by human capacities. The person who escorts the nephrite is unique and alone. To escort a new consignment of nephrite, he has to take rest in the city and then go back to the mine, and this takes more time than a single nephrite trip. The man plays here the role of a filter that constrains the capacity of the channel to transfer the nephrite. This is an important point that distinguishes the nephrite road from the supply chains that operate in the modern capitalistic world with their ceaseless flow of goods and disconnectedness of humans.

1 Nephrite is transported from the mine to the bank of the river. The mine is situated on the other side of the big river. And there are only two all-terrain vehicles that run between the mine and the big river. This trip takes 2-3 hours. Only a special amphibious all-terrain vehicle can cross the river, all other vehicles can cross the river only at specially designated points and at infrequent and particular times.

2 There is a special post at the bank, where only one person lives permanently. He has a boat and helps to connect the two banks. Recently the community has bought a special amphibious all-terrain vehicle and people have to conduct fewer crossings where the nephrite is reloaded from the all-terrain vehicles on the one side of the river onto the vehicles that wait for the load on the other side of the river.

3 The trip between the river and the next station takes approximately 6 hours. This is the most difficult part of the territory, with mountains, rivers and changing landscape. Usually there are five vehicles that form the caravan. The station where they stop is the reindeer farm, where people eat and have some short rest. After an hour they start again toward the next station.

4 The huge truck goes to the city. On its way it stops at some places, firstly at the picnic site but only for a short smoking break. This is the last stop within the territories where all people that can be met are somehow connected with the nephrite community.

5 The next station is the last stop for the all-terrain vehicles. From then on there is a hard paved motor road. The load from all five all-terrain vehicles is reloaded onto one huge dumping truck. This station is the place where all the transport needs are serviced, checked and fixed. Here main workshops and stores holding spare parts and lubricants are situated, as well as fuel tanks.

6 The last possible stop for the truck, which is usually is omitted, is at the old station of the community at the central village. The truck crosses the village to enter the main motor road. Recently this station has only been used as a reserve station for emergency situations and to store supplies. Between the central village and the town, where the nephrite is stored in the warehouses of the main station, the truck stops several times at private canteens, where people have food and a very short rest. The trip between the village and the town takes 12 hours.

1

3

2

4

5

6

7

3. Canteens

There are two basic sources of energy that drive things and maintain the channel of the nephrite road: the metabolism of human beings and the fuel burning inside various engines. Canteens are places to support the human capacity to act. Every station has various canteens, from the simplest self-service spaces to complex canteens with kitchens and special staff. All-terrain vehicles bring food supplies and fuel on their way back to the mine, and all these substances are distributed between the stations and are consumed in the taiga. But all stations try to integrate and process local food stuffs as well, and through these additions make their food more delicious, nutritious and interesting. Supplies that are delivered contain dry staple foods (such as rice, flour and macaroni) and various canned goods, some limited amount of vegetables, sweets and cookies. What people add to their diet from local natural environments are fresh meat, fish, and berries. Some people grow their own vegetables as well. All people who live in the taiga participate in such food gathering. At some stations, food processing is regulated by a stable ongoing regime, at other stations food for the members of the nephrite caravan is cooked occasionally and specifically for them. In comparison to the vehicles that simply need fuel, people's efficacy depends not only on the amounts of the food, but also on its variability and taste. Good moods are dependent on the type of food people eat, especially in the forest, where food is not only a source of nourishment, but also the main form of entertainment. Food products from the taiga never arrive on a pre-planned basis and always surprise and delight people. They are the most impressive entertainment of all. Forest food (whether the meat of wild roe or salted mushrooms) always has the potency to become an event and a reason for a feast at the station. Through such food the surrounding environment intrudes into the core circuits of energies, thoughts and emotions of the nephrite road. The nephrite road is not a sterile tube. Such encroachments of the environment upon the channel of the nephrite road are very much welcomed by people. These constitute, so to speak, pleasant noises.

1 There is a special canteen at the mine, where all workers and caravan drivers eat at regular hours. But people who live in the forest for half the year also cook for themselves to sustain the pleasure of autonomy. They do simple things, such as making tea, for which they may have no special pots. The glass jar which serves both as a pot and a cup at once shows the simplicity and asceticism of their life-style.

2 The most elaborate kitchen household is maintained at the station, where the nephrite rocks are reloaded from the all-terrain vehicles onto the truck. Here there is even a green-house for growing cucumbers and other delicacies.

3 Wild roe is occasionally killed by drivers of the all-terrain vehicles. Meat is processed at the next station on their route.

4 The facilities of the canteen are used for private purposes also, for example, when the caravan leaves, and passengers who came with the caravan vehicles stay and produce bottles of vodka that they have brought as presents to the station keepers. The canteen is transformed into into a place to hold a party.

5 At the reindeer camp, which is also used as a place to have lunch, the approaching caravan is heard 30 minutes before it actually arrives. This is the time that people at the station have to prepare food for the caravan members. This imposes a condition that at this camp people eat only such foods as can be cooked in 30 minutes - usually boiled buckwheat served with tinned stewed meat.

6 In contrast to the reindeer camp, the next station is almost always ready to receive drivers and workers. Food that is served here is diverse and consists of several dishes.

7 The kitchen is fully equipped, and the cook maintains various pots and crockery in complex and functional order.

1

2

3

4

5

6

4. Wires

Systems of wires are part of almost all stations, where people permanently live. Electricity is energy that helps to maintain the work of the station. Electricity is generated from the fuel that is used to fill up the tanks of the all-terrain vehicles. Special generators work several hours each day. There is no single electricity system that encompasses the nephrite route, but islands of electricity between which people and vehicles move. Wires and hoses are channels for the circulation of energy, gases and information. The nephrite road can be thought of as such a wire through which the information and substances circulate. Wires connect the various buildings of the station into a system of places where people can live and accomplish tasks. Electricity is used mainly to light the rooms and power equipment, such as the turning machine, but also to power washing machines and pumps in households. Electricity is part of the nephrite road and appeared in this region only after the nephrite road started to operate. Some stations that were included into the nephrite road had existed before. At that time there was no electricity network, no generators and fuel supplies at these camps. Ultimately electricity in the taiga is generated from the stone that is driven from the mountain to the city and on its way generates the difference in value that is then transformed into cash, then fuel and only then into electricity. The nephrite road is a complex power station that turns stones into light.

1 The electricity system of the nephrite mine is local and looks different from the power lines with concrete poles that we are accustomed to seeing. This electricity system does not belong to the state and has a different appearance. It looks fragile and temporary, although it has been working for several years already. Every year people change most of the details and wires, which does not usually happen with the power lines operated by the state.

2 To reduce the noise that the power generator creates, people have built special constructions almost under the ground and enclose the generators inside. But still the sound of the generator can clearly be heard, and it is always very well known if the generator works, and if there is electricity at the station at a particular time. This noisiness of electricity provides a distinctive character which is local and not vast and owned by state power system.

3 At the station where people make intensive use of electricity in the transport repair workshops, there is a certain voltage standard that is needed for the working of equipment. At this station the electricity line looks very solid and almost as it would look if it were a state power line.

4 Wires are connected and these connections are openly displayed, because people do not need the illusion that everything is under control simply because it is not seen. On the contrary, to maintain control over the electrical system, people need to see all the joint points and to know how and where wires are connected.

5 The workshop is a place that can work only with electricity supply.

6 Some equipment, such as an automatic gas-welding machine does not need electricity, but gas, that is concentrated in the gas cylinder and flows through the hose.

1

2

3

4

5

6

5. Buildings

Stations are growing. Every season new buildings are built and new infrastructures are added. This makes people's lives easier and more comfortable. This development of stations is an effect of their networking. The successful advances in one station are implemented in the others. This growth is also a result of interaction between local station workers and members of the central office that from time to time come to the stations to evaluate the work and approve developments. This communication is mainly focused on the approval of recently built projects and the generation of new ones. The check-up is the situation where this exchange happens. Building, checking up the quality of the work and providing new plans are actions that mingle with each other and any work done is always done in the context of future plans. In this respect we can say that stations as units are active growers themselves, because plans for new buildings are usually generated on the local level during the building process, and only during the check-ups are these plans transferred to the controlling personnel. The latter reformulate these plans later as tasks and send them to stations with the necessary materials and equipments. Old facilities that lose their usefulness are sometimes left as ruins, but usually they are demolished and the materials are reused, either as building materials for minor constructions or as fuel. The life and development of stations is a circuit process in which all elements continue on going through collision with each other. There are several such meeting points during the season, when stations are visited by controlling personnel of various rank, from the head of the development department to the head of the community.

1-2 During construction, breaks for rest are used to observe the developed area. People talk about their work, and what to do next. They discuss not only short term plans, but also how what they do fits the possibilities to build new sites. They think of how their actions affect the possibility to connect buildings with the electric system and other communal facilities. There is no common unitary plan according to which stations are developed.

3 New buildings coexist with old ones. Construction and demolition are sometimes parallel.

4 All plans (realized and future) are articulated during the main check-up, when closer to the end of the extracting season, the head of the community travels along the nephrite road and visits all the stations. This is an important and happy moment, when people meet each other and share their plans and achievements.

5 The head of the department for development points out defects and orders them to be fixed. This does not simply apply to one particular problem, but it is also an opportunity to evaluate the whole project, add new constructive decisions, and think about the future changes.

6 During the check-up and approval of the newly-built house, people discuss the possible new projects that would fit with this house. These could be drainage constructions or additional pathways and bridges, but also other buildings. All these plans that people discuss openly in front of the senior management will later become tasks for them to realize.

1

2

3

4

5

6

7

6. Repair

Mechanized systems are mostly not capable of repairing their failures themselves, but the human-machine systems can do it. People repair vehicles and do it with the help of other engines and instruments. Stations are the places where such mechanistic regeneration happens. In this respect the nephrite road is a self-correcting system that not only grows but also self-repairs. The main objects of repair are vehicles that are the elements of the nephrite road most intensively exposed to contact with the environment. Parts of vehicles wear out and need to be repeatedly replaced by new ones. Most fragile are the wheels and caterpillar tracks that are in direct contact with the earth when vehicles go through forests. Other fragile points are the engines that require cleaning and the servicing of various contacts in their electric systems. What people struggle with, or try to eliminate the effects of, in the workshop is friction. Vehicles move through a world that resists. Repair is the resistance of humans to the resistance of machines to the resistance of the environment. Repair is an attempt to bridge these various forms of friction and balance them. It is important to note that people spend half of their work time on repairs. Sometimes they have to wait for spare parts ordered from the city, but very frequently they repair these parts by themselves, cut new parts or assemble parts from the engines that were previously rejected as irreparable. During the repair some vehicles are rejected, and become part of the debris that surrounds the workshops to provide the materials for repairs of other more reparable vehicles.

1 The rough grinding machine is a useful piece of equipment. With this tool people sharpen other instruments, such as knives, but also clear rust from the surfaces of the parts.

2 The turning lathe helps in cutting new parts from the raw materials.

3 With the gas welding unit, people can assemble the different components of parts together.

4 The workshop is a space that is covered by spare parts and tools. This is a collection of the workshop that exists as an active display. Tools are taken out of their places, used and put back.

5 During the repair the vehicles are turned inside out. The engines and other subsystems of the vehicles are separated from each other and displayed as detached elements. But at the same time, all these parts are left close to the vehicle. During the repair the vehicle is not the system of its elements, but a collection of its parts.

6 Wheels are parts that are designed to be relatively easily changed and repaired. The replacement of wheels is an ordinary and routine task.

7 Spare parts are taken from a broken and irreparable vehicle.

1

2

3

4

5

6

7

8

7. Debris of Rubbish

Stations are surrounded by rubbish. This debris forms an important feature of the landscape; the buffer and the contact zone between nature and the nephrite road. Things that become part of this debris have usually been crushed by the natural environment. Some are vehicles and iron constructions that have been broken to such an extent that people could not repair them, but there are also things that have lost their usefulness due to wider environmental and infrastructural changes, such as market changes or the introduction of new, more efficient models of vehicles. Slowly the debris of rubbish is sorted out. Those elements that can be recycled are used by people to repair things that are parts of the nephrite road. Those which remain are covered with soil and other natural substances, and become part of the natural environment. The smaller items are usually recycled and reutilized by people, while at the same time the larger components of the rubbish debris stay visible. As a result, the rubbish debris looks mostly like heaps of big metal remnants, left to become rusty. The rubbish debris shows how fast metal things change under the influence of environment if left unattended by people. The corrosion and deformation of the left-over things is irreversible and its speed is quite fast. People struggle with these processes, constantly repairing their vehicles. The debris shows to what extent their efforts are important to maintain the nephrite road working.

1 The water cannon once was used for washing gold, when the community was extracting gold from the soil of the gold mines that belonged to it. Since the nephrite trade became more profitable, gold mining was resumed, but the water cannon was left unused. Without care it quickly turned into rusty trash.

2 The broken crane firstly was separated from its wheeled platform, which was used for other purposes, and then it turned into a grand object of rejection. Ironically to remove the abandoned crane, people need to use the new crane that, in time, will also be abandoned

3 Our young assistant has collected various clocks that once belonged to different pieces of equipment in the rubbish debris that surrounds the station. This variety shows how many different functions these items of machinery have been used for. All these clocks were intended to measure pressures of various substances under multiple conditions.

4 Some strange frames sometimes can be seen in the debris. For example, this automobile body was probably driven here to be fixed at the repair workshops. But this unique chance did not help this machine creature to avoid its fate of becoming a part of the rubbish debris.

5 Old models of all-terrain vehicles can be found stripped of their most valuable materials and elements – windows and caterpillar crawlers.

6 Several examples of newer all-terrain vehicle models form a kind of geological layer in the debris of rubbish. This layer designates the evidence of the first successes of the community and the start of its prosperity phase, when it bought and changed its first cohort of all-terrain vehicles.

7 Wheels from all-terrain vehicles are also fragile elements that need to be changed from time to time. The deformed wheels can be frequently seen, left in the debris.

8 Other replaceable elements are the caterpillar crawlers that are changed several times during a season. As a result, there are many cracked caterpillar tracks left in the vicinity of the station.

1

2

3

4

5

6

7

8

8. Caterpillars and wheels

The wheels of the all-terrain vehicles do not run on the ground but on the closed chains of their caterpillars. We can say that these caterpillars are the roads for the vehicles. The road is part of a machine; when wheels turn, they not only push the vehicle further, but they also push the road back, but for caterpillars that rotation is closed within the wheels. All-terrain vehicles do not need a road to go through territory. The caterpillars leave traces on the ground they pass and at the same time caterpillars sustain the friction in the places where the ground is too strong to leave a trace. The infrastructure of the nephrite road consists of stations that are connected by all-terrain vehicles. There are no roads between the stations, only traces of the caterpillars that mark where the all-terrain vehicles usually pass. But these traces do not make the territory easier to go through. On the contrary, drivers usually have to bypass the traces, because it is easier to go upon the untouched ground. Caterpillars have to be replaced several times during the season. Instead of building roads, people change the caterpillars on their all-terrain vehicles. This not only reduces the cost of the nephrite road, but also makes it almost impossible for other people to use the infrastructure of the nephrite road. Exceptions are made only for those who have their own all-terrain vehicles, which are very expensive to maintain and supply with petrol. Helicopter access is possible but extremely expensive and only an option in exceptional circumstances for senior community officials or state organizations. The all-terrain vehicle is autonomous, it does not need a road to pass through the territory, but it needs to be repaired and filled up with petroleum from time to time. This relative autonomy of the all-terrain vehicle, in comparison to other more widely used means of transport such as ordinary cars, makes the nephrite road secure from intrusion, and more autonomous itself. All the elements of the nephrite road, including stations and all-terrain vehicles, need only to be in contact with each other for comparatively short periods and infrequently. The work of the infrastructure of the nephrite road does not need ever-present communication and coordination. All channels are used to their lowest capacity without transferring extra messages or extra loads.

1 The truck has brought new caterpillars for the excavators that are used at the mine and wheels for all-terrain vehicles. These are the parts that need to be regularly replaced.

2 For transportation purposes the caterpillars are rolled up.

3 Often people change caterpillars and front wheels at the same time on the assumption that these parts struggle with the same level of friction.

4 To change caterpillars the vehicles move forward and back. The caterpillar chains are disconnected and at particular moments the all-terrain vehicle runs on its wheels directly touching the ground, without the mediation of the caterpillars.

5 Some local people have their own all-terrain vehicles. Usually these are very old models that have been repaired by people many times. This model is from the end of 1950s.

6 All-terrain vehicles are designed to make use of the friction. The vehicle cannot be moved from the place without its engines turning the wheels. This makes the vehicle very stable. The vehicle itself is also very heavy and this increases the pressure on the caterpillars.

7 Muddy places are easily traversed by all-terrain vehicles. Vehicles can be stuck sometimes, but the caterpillars are rarely broken in such places.

8 Rocks are the main cause of the caterpillars' tear and wear.

1

2

3

4

5

6

7

8

9. Caterpillars and terrain

Caterpillars are in contact with the ground and protect the wheels, whose function is reduced to rotation. To turn the vehicle, the driver can set different speeds of rotation for the wheels. If the wheels on the right side turn faster than on the left side, the vehicle turns right. The driver uses the brakes that are situated on the two levers that correspond to the right and left caterpillar. The control of the all-terrain vehicle is based on digital information as opposed to the analogous principle of the steering wheel of the ordinary car. Friction is used for the movement and is not interpreted as just a disturbance and obstacle for the movement. The all-terrain vehicle either changes the place where it goes or is changed by the place and broken. But to move forward the all-terrain vehicle needs contact with the ground and the more points it contacts, the more efficiently it can use the friction that it produces. In this respect, the situations that are most dangerous are those when the vehicle is not resting on its caterpillars, but is stuck and for some reason there is not enough contact with the ground. For example, when the vehicle is in a depression, and because of vertical inclination the weight of the vehicle is unevenly distributed. The caterpillars are not pressed by the vehicle's weight to the ground along all their contact zones and the vehicle cannot extricate itself from the dip.. But as long as the caterpillars manage to find more contact with the terrain, the level of friction grows and the vehicle can take itself out. The main principle of the autonomy of the all-terrain vehicle is its openness to the contacts with the surfaces. This is the paradox of its autonomy, which is opposite to the idea of the vehicle that uses the road. In the latter scheme the moving body is meant to reduce its contact with the surface to a minimum. The all-terrain vehicle principle of searching for the contact with the environment so as to enforce the autonomy from this environment is the principle that dominates the organization of the nephrite road on all levels of its management and function.

1 An all-terrain vehicle is stuck. It is attempting to traverse the invisible stones that stick up from under the water. These stones are polished by water and are slippery. The heavy vehicle cannot find enough friction to move off these stones.

2 To widen the contact of the caterpillars with the ground and increase the friction, people put tree trunks under the caterpillars. So that through the destruction of these trunks, the vehicle gets itself out from its stationary position on the stones.

3 The crossing of shallow rivers wears the caterpillars out, because of the small stones that stick up. When the vehicle runs upon them, the distribution of its mass on the caterpillars is uneven, which though it does not break them immediately, damages them in the long term.

4 Tracks in the mountain forests that are intensively used by all-terrain vehicles look like river beds, because vehicles tear off the earth and leave the stones exposed. These processes of erosion are accelerated by rains and the water that start to collect along these tracks. All-terrain vehicles trespass the territory they traverse to the limits of their own possibility to pass through it. Slowly they turn the territory into a landscape which is dangerous for themselves.

5 But firstly all-terrain vehicles turn spaces into mud, which is the most comfortable surface to travel through for the caterpillars and the wheels that rotate them.

6 Places that are used for stops of the all-terrain vehicles rapidly turn into muddy bogs. For example, stations are surrounded by bogs because these are the places where all-terrain vehicles concentrate. Constructed to pass through muddy terrains, all-terrain vehicles turn their environment into such terrains as a result.

7 All-terrain vehicles are not supposed to use ordinary roads, because either they destroy the surfaces of the roads, or they suffer themselves because of the stones that are used to firm up the road surfaces.

8 The use of all-terrain vehicles makes the territory where they are used even more impassable. The infrastructure that is based around the all-terrain vehicles is impossible to use without all-terrain vehicles.

1

2

3

4

5

6

7

8

10. Stops

On their way between stations, the all-terrain vehicles make short stops. Drivers collect water to cool down the engines. People have a short rest, smoke and chat. People rest from the noise of the engines that almost prevents any conversations on the way. The pitching and rolling which occurs during the trip is intensive and very tiring. The short stops are moments of calmness and tranquility. During the trip people sit either inside the cabin or outside in the body. There is almost no possibility during the trip to maintain contact between people and to interact. All the forces need to be concentrated and devoted to maintaining the posture and avoiding blows over the sides of the vehicle. At the same time, the only person that has control over the situation is the driver, and all others are passive passengers. Only the driver knows the possibilities of his vehicle to pass the obstacles, and only he has the capacity to react in time. These distinctions in resources and available information, and the need to actively experience the road even without the necessity to, act block the interaction between fellow travelers, and it is only during the short stops that the interaction between them resumes. During these stops people get out of the vehicle and find themselves inside territories that they would not otherwise intrude into. There are hundreds of square kilometers of uninhabited land, and probably without the all-terrain vehicle that has brought them there they would not be able to walk here by themselves. If anything happens to the vehicle, the walk to the closest station can take a day and it would be a very difficult task as there is no road except for the muddy traces of the all-terrain vehicle and no bridges on the rivers. During these stops people do not go far away from the vehicles and usually they spend most of the time chatting, standing in a circle, looking at each other, sharing comments about issues of common interest. These spontaneous circles are surprising in their organizational simplicity and obviousness. People are not being confused in their use of such an egalitarian pattern in their interaction. There is no centre and no focus for the collective interaction, but the ability to see everybody and the ability to say whatever you want to everybody. These stops are comfortable moments of sociability in the flow of noise and chaotic swaying in the vehicle during the hours of a trip.

1 Usually the caravan of all-terrain vehicles stops at the bank of the river to drink fresh water and collect water for engines.

2 A circle of people smoking and chatting.

3 Accidents are moments when people have to stay in the taiga until they manage to resolve the problem. Usually, people who cannot help and can only wait form the same circles for chatting and smoking.

4 Sometimes people wait in the taiga for others to come. This can continue for hours and most of the time people maintain the same circles.

5 If the stop happens in a muddy place and people do not want to step down from the vehicles onto the ground, they improvise circles of chatting and smoking on the vehicles themselves. They open the cabin's hatches and stand on the steps.

6 Sometimes people can find a bounty of berries right beside the place where the vehicles have stopped.

7 The caravan, with a truck transporting a petrol tank and a bus carrying people, stopped for a short rest. People go from the city to the first station, which is situated on the edge of the taiga. The surroundings are not so wild and uninhabited, and people do not feel the need to spend this stop in a circle.

8 But sometimes the circle order emerges during trips on the road. This happens if people know each other well and this is the beginning of their journey to the taiga. Members of this circle will spend several of the coming days in each other's company, changing from cars to the all-terrain vehicles and making long stops at stations and short stops at river banks.

1

2

3

4

5

6

7

8

11. Docking

The infrastructure of the nephrite road is built and developed to sustain the flow of nephrite from the mine to the city warehouse. In the course of this, nephrite is reloaded several times from different forms of transport. These moments can be compared to docking in space, when the atmosphere of one transport is open to the atmosphere of the other transport, with the only difference that the atmospheres that we are talking about here do not consist of air, but of the mood, or the way people experience these forms of transport as reliable and comfortable, as opposed to the outer space of the taiga, which is the world of vacuum without comfort and reliability. Although docking presupposes the attempt to build a corridor and exclude the surrounding environment, the operation itself happens in the environment and successful docking is always based on an attentive work with the environment. Because different types of transport are constructed for moving in different terrains, docking is the moment when these specialized capacities have to be connected, and this can happen only in the places where these terrains meet as well. Usually different modes of transport have different capacities. This means that to reload nephrite from the transport with bigger capacity the transport with lower capacity needs to connect several times with the first one, and vice versa. And usually the transport with the bigger capacity plays the role of the port, and other types of transport are connected to it and then either carry away their loads and come back for new portions, or are interchanged with other small vehicles that carry new portions of nephrite to upload onto the big truck. Connection needs to be calibrated and people use gestures to show the drivers how to park their vehicles as close as possible to a bigger truck.

1 In order to connect with the boat onto which the nephrite will be loaded to transport it to the other side of the river, where it will be uploaded on another all-terrain vehicle, this all-terrain vehicle needs to ride into the water. This is a dangerous intrusion for the vehicle into an unfriendly terrain, where it could get stuck trying to traverse invisible stones.

2 Finally the docking is done and the boat is attached to the vehicle, fixed by a rope.

3 People start to load the boat. The nephrite rocks are very heavy, but they need to be carefully put into the boat, not thrown, so as to avoid rolling and unbalancing the boat.

4 Although there is still space on the boat to load more nephrite, the upper limit of the boat's capacity to accept it is reached. Nephrite is very heavy. The boat has to conduct a number of trips across the river to empty one all-terrain vehicle.

5 One big truck can transport the total amount of nephrite that is carried by six all-terrain vehicles. At the last taiga station the caravan of all-terrain vehicles is unloaded. Loaders station themselves inside the body of the truck, standing upon the nephrite rocks that have just been loaded.

6 When the two bodies of the truck and all-terrain vehicle are adjusted, people pass onto the all-terrain vehicle side.

7 Nephrite rocks are thrown one by one from the all-terrain vehicle into the truck body.

8 The all-terrain vehicle is situated on a gradient so as to be of the same height as the truck. Drivers stay outside their vehicles. Their work is done for the moment. The security guard observes the operation from above. Loading workers are busy in the all-terrain vehicle side of the dock. Nephrite flows. As soon as this all-terrain vehicle is emptied, the next vehicle will take its place at the dock.

1

2

3

4

5

6

12. Environment

Although the aim of most efforts is a minimization of contacts with the environment, these contacts are unavoidable, firstly, because nephrite is a part of the environment and, secondly, because the environment is not a stable category but a relative one. This means that everything that is part of the nephrite road can, at some point, become a part of the environment, like the carcasses of the vehicles it was not possible to repair and continue to use. Without a regular flow of nephrite, stations will rapidly become empty camps, with decaying buildings; traces of all-terrain vehicles will slowly disappear; the dynamited areas of the nephrite mountain will be covered by soil and new plants. All these processes will take time, but at some point it will be very difficult to distinguish the shapes of the ruins of the nephrite road from other natural features of the landscape. This has already happened with the numerous gold mines that operated in the region ten years ago, and now are left abandoned. However wild and uninhabited the region looks, it has been intensively exploited by people for more than two hundred years, and traces of this intrusion can be found everywhere, albeit that these traces become part of the environment and as such are difficult to spot. From this perspective we can say that the environment per se is nothing else but the ruins of other previously existing channels that were delivering other messages, such as gold, fur or other valuables. The environment is a noise that consists of fragments of these undelivered messages. The decay and destruction that the nephrite road causes to its environment are also parts of that environment, not only as extra elements or refuse additions, but also as an internal quality of the environment itself. The capacity of the environment to regenerate is also a logical consequence of its ability to be destroyed. The nephrite road is an ongoing process of destruction of the environment, through polluting rivers, leaving traces, and intensifying erosion, as well as generating noise. These various forms of pollution are counterbalanced by the ability of the environment to become more and more uncomfortable to people and at the same time to encompass new landscapes as its part. Whatever people do, the nephrite road cannot be isolated from its environment and when people try to maintain the channel through which nephrite flows without friction they create a paradoxical task. Noise is an unavoidable part of the channel, because to some extent it is the only material that is at hand to make the channel. And a piece of information that is a message sent through this channel is a fraction of noise too. Nephrite is part of the environment sent through the environment. And even people who feel so uncomfortable in this environment are an integral part of it. The nephrite road is a unique flow that changes the life of the taiga, people and nephrite, like any other strong flow or river that changes the territory it flows through.

1 View from the nephrite mountain.

2 The river that changes the environment.

3 The steppe is an easy place to cross on the all-terrain vehicle, but almost impossible to cross otherwise, because of its fragile and smooth surface. It quickly becomes a dangerous quagmire underfoot.

4 Burnt trees are the traces of forest fires. It is impossible to say whether these fires were set by humans or occurred naturally. The destruction is a process that does not have to be initiated by an agency or controlled by the agency.

5 Even the small rivers are strewn with trees that have been flushed downstream and have become part of the natural detritus that forms their banks.

6 These green hills are heaps of sand excavated and washed by people in the search for gold. There is still much gold here, but it is dispersed and the gold particles are so small that to extract them from the sand people have to apply new technologies that are based on chemical reactions. At this time, the reagents are too expensive, but the time will come when the market will change, and people will return to these abandoned heaps of sand and will rediscover them. New forms of pollution will change this environment that at the moment looks like it has almost recovered from the earlier intrusions.

Alexandra Lavrillier and Semen Gabyshev

An Arctic Indigenous Knowledge System
of Landscape, Climate, and Human Interactions:
Evenki Reindeer Herders and Hunters

2017, Fürstenberg/Havel: Kulturstiftung Sibirien
ca. 470 pp., ca. 300 color photos, 15,5 x 22 cm
ISBN: 978-3-942883-31-3
Euro 68; paperback

Studies in Social and Cultural Anthropology
https://dh-north.org/digitale-bibliothek/studies-in-social-and-cultural-anthropology/en

---

Erich Kasten and Raisa Avak (eds.)

Одежда и прикладное искусство эвенов Быстринского района / Clothing and Decorative Arts, Evens, Bystrinski district

2018, Fürstenberg/Havel: Kulturstiftung Sibirien
277 pp., 15,5 x 22 cm
ISBN: 978-3-942883-20-7
Euro 18, paperback | DVD, 3:58 hrs.: Euro 28

Languages and Cultures of the Russian Far East
https://dh-north.org/digitale-bibliothek/languages-and-cultures-of-the-russian-far-east/en

---

Erich Kasten (ed.)

Духовная культура коряков-нымыланов с. Лесная, Камчатка: Мировоззрения и ритуальные праздники Worldviews and Ritual Practice, Coastal Koryaks (Nymylans), Lesnaya, Kamchatka.

2017, Fürstenberg/Havel: Kulturstiftung Sibirien
168 pp.,15,5 x 22 cm
ISBN: 978-3-942883-32-0
Euro 18, paperback | DVD, 2:25 hrs.: Euro 28

Languages and Cultures of the Russian Far East
https://dh-north.org/digitale-bibliothek/languages-and-cultures-of-the-russian-far-east/en

---

Stephan Dudeck

Der Tag des Rentierzüchters:
Repräsentation indigener Lebensstile
zwischen Taigawohnplatz und Erdölstadt in Westsibirien

2013, Fürstenberg/Havel: Kulturstiftung Sibirien
351 pp., 20 color photos, 15,5 x 22 cm
ISBN: 978-3-942883-17-7
Euro 34, paperback

Studies in Social and Cultural Anthropology
https://dh-north.org/digitale-bibliothek/studies-in-social-and-cultural-anthropology/en

---

Bulgakova, Tatiana

Nanai Shamanic Culture
in Indigenous Discourse

2013, Fürstenberg/Havel: Kulturstiftung Sibirien
264 pp., 15,5 x 22 cm, 5 color photos
Euro 28; paperback
ISBN: 978-3-942883-14-6

Studies in Social and Cultural Anthropology
https://dh-north.org/digitale-bibliothek/studies-in-social-and-cultural-anthropology/en

---

Erich Kasten and Tjeerd de Graaf (eds.)

Sustaining Indigenous Knowledge:
Learning Tools and Community Initiatives for
Preserving EndangeredLanguages and Local Cultural Heritage

2013, Fürstenberg/Havel: Kulturstiftung Sibirien
284 pp., 22 color photos, 15,5 x 22 cm
ISBN: 978-3-942883-12-2
Euro 26; paperback

Exhibitions and Symposia
https://dh-north.org/digitale-bibliothek/exhibitions-and-symposia/en

---